APRON FULL OF GOLD

MARY JANE MEGQUIER, BEFORE 1849 [1993].

APRON FULL OF
GOLD

THE LETTERS OF MARY JANE MEGQUIER
FROM SAN FRANCISCO
1849–1856

SECOND EDITION
EDITED & WITH AN INTRODUCTION BY
POLLY WELTS KAUFMAN

INTRODUCTION TO THE FIRST EDITION BY
ROBERT GLASS CLELAND

UNIVERSITY OF NEW MEXICO PRESS
ALBUQUERQUE

Library of Congress Cataloging-in-Publication Data

Megquier, Mary Jane, 1813–1899.
　　Apron full of gold : the letters of Mary Jane Megquier from San
Francisco, 1849–1856 / edited by Robert Glass Cleland : introduction
by Polly Welts Kaufman. — 2nd ed.
　　p.　cm.
　　Includes index.
　　ISBN 0–8263–1500–3 (paperback)
　　1. Voyages to the Pacific Coast. 2. California—Gold discoveries.
3. Frontier and pioneer life—California. 4. Magquier, Mary Jane,
1813–1899—Correspondence. 5. Pioneers–California—Correspondence.
6. Woman pioneer—California—Correspondence.　I. Cleland, Robert
Glass, 1885–1957.　II. Title.
F865.M45　1994
979.4'6104'092—dc20　　　　　　　　　　　　　　93–29907
[B}　　　　　　　　　　　　　　　　　　　　　　　CIP

Designed by Linda Mae Tratechaud

FOR LINDY & HEIDI

C O N T E N T S

ILLUSTRATIONS / IX
INTRODUCTION TO THE SECOND EDITION
POLLY WELTS KAUFMAN / XI

INTRODUCTION TO THE FIRST EDITION
ROBERT GLASS CLELAND / XXVII

CHAPTER I. FIRST JOURNEY:
From Maine to San Francisco via Panama,
December 1848 to January 1851
—Mary Jane Megquier & Thomas L. Megquier / 1

CHAPTER II. SECOND JOURNEY:
To San Francisco via Nicaragua,
April 1852 to March 1854
—Mary Jane Megquier & Thomas L. Megquier / 75

CHAPTER III. THIRD JOURNEY:
San Francisco, November 1855 to June 1856
—Mary Jane Megquier / 139

Index / 169

ILLUSTRATIONS

MARY JANE MEGQUIER, BEFORE 1849,
FROM A DAGUERREOTYPE [1993] / FRONTISPIECE

NEEDLEWORK BY MARY JANE COLE [MEGQUIER], 1824 [1993] / XIII

FOUR GENERATIONS OF COLE WOMEN, ABOUT 1856,
FROM A GLASS NEGATIVE [1993] / XXII

PORTABLE IRON HOUSE, ADVERTISEMENT IN J.E. SHERWOOD'S
POCKET GUIDE TO CALIFORNIA, 1849 / 5

THOMAS L. AND MARY JANE MEGQUIER, FROM A DAGUERREOTYPE,
EARLY 1850S [1993] / 11

ANGELINE, JOHN OTIS, AND ARTHUR SELWYN MEGQUIER,
FROM A DAGUERREOTYPE, EARLY 1850S [1993] / 18

VIEW OF SAN FRANCISCO, FEBRUARY 1850,
LETTERHEAD LITHOGRAPHED IN GOLD / 51

GREAT FIRE IN SAN FRANCISCO, MAY 4, 1850,
LITHOGRAPHED LETTERHEAD / 54

EXECUTION OF JOSÉ FORNI, DECEMBER 10, 1852,
LITHOGRAPHED LETTERHEAD / 111

LOLA HAS COME! CONTEMPORARY LITHOGRAPH / 128

GILSON AND MEGQUIER FAMILIES, FROM A DAGUERREOTYPE,
1854 [1993] / 134

BREAKFASTING ON SHORE, LITHOGRAPH FROM LETTS,
PICTORIAL VIEW OF CALIFORNIA, 1853 / 142

BEECHCROFT, WINTHROP, ME, 1854 [1993] / 144

SURRENDER OF JAMES P. CASEY AND CHARLES CORA,
PRINTED LETTEREHAD, MAY 18, 1856 / 160

CHINESE SEWING BOX, GIFT TO BETTIE AND MILTON BENJAMIN,
1850S [1993] / 164

INTRODUCTION

TO THE SECOND EDITION

POLLY WELTS KAUFMAN

The Gold Rush letters written by Mary Jane Megquier recounting her experiences in San Francisco and her three journeys across Central America to California and back are a remarkable chronicle of the extraordinary efforts of a wife and husband from Maine to make their fortune. The letters also reveal the physical and emotional costs of their enterprise. In addition, the Megquiers' story documents the process by which Mary Jane Megquier, in particular, arrived at the difficult decision of whether to stay in California with its promise of a freer society or to return to traditional life in New England.

When Robert Glass Cleland first edited the letters in 1949 during the centennial of the Gold Rush, his purpose was to present the response of "two ordinary Americans from a restricted provincial background" to an "unconventional society." In order not to detract from Mary Jane Megquier's candid and often pithy descriptions of life in mid-nineteenth-century San Francisco and her journeys to California, he omitted passages in the letters that he considered personal with "no historical significance." He also left out most of the few surviving letters written by Mary Jane Megquier's husband, Dr. Thomas L. Megquier, who was her partner in the venture.[1]

Since 1949 and after more than two decades of publishing in women's history, historians are finding new significance in historical documents written by women about their experiences in the American West. In particular, some historians believe that only by identifying the difference between a woman's and a man's perceptions of their life experiences can women's stories be accurately told. By omitting the personal and familial passages in the Megquier letters, Cleland presented the experiences of Mary Jane Megquier and her husband as a unit without distinguishing between their different points of view. But because they were socialized differently from birth and played different roles both in New England and in California, Mary Jane and Thomas Megquier's perceptions of their experiences were often different from one another's. It was this difference that undoubtedly led to their eventual separation.[2]

This new edition of Mary Jane Megquier's letters from San Francisco and Central America restores the personal and familial passages omitted from the first edition. It also includes several notes and letters from Thomas Megquier previously unpublished. The details of the Megquiers' journeys across Central America and of life in San Francisco between 1849 and 1856 still illuminate the pioneer experience of American women and men and provide an excellent resource for social historians. When examined in their entirety, however, the letters prove to be an even more useful source for women's history. Only then can the reader ascertain how Mary Jane Megquier's entire western experience, coupled with the values and familial ties she brought with her from the East, influenced her behavior and affected her decisions. Her authentic voice can now be heard.

The letters provide an example of a woman in mid-nineteenth-century America who embraced modernism and rejected the constraints of New England small-town life and who worked to provide the economic support needed to insure her family's upward mobility in a changing world. They also demonstrate the enormous cost to a woman who endured a painful separation from those very family members she intended to help. The Megquiers, as did others who participated in the Gold Rush, showed their love for their children by taking unusual measures to provide for their financial support. Yet, for Mary Jane Megquier, having to put the economic well being of her children above their emotional and social needs created severe conflicts within her. Thomas Megquier, on the other hand,

NEEDLEWORK BY MARY JANE COLE [MEGQUIER] AT THE AGE OF
ELEVEN IN 1824 [1993].

remained convinced that his primary duty was to provide for his children's financial welfare.

Both Mary Jane and Thomas Megquier were well acquainted with the exigencies and restrictions of farm life in south central Maine. Born Mary Jane Cole on December 11, 1813, she was brought up on her family's farm in Turner, a town about fifteen miles west of Winthrop, where her father, Nathan Cole, was born in 1786. From her mother, Rebecca Pollard Cole, who was born in 1791, Mary Jane learned the many skills that would allow her to be successful at running boarding houses in San Francisco. She also became accomplished in sewing and dressmaking. A well-crafted piece of needlework created by Mary Jane when she was only eleven is reproduced here. The one surviving note from Rebecca Cole shows that she was literate although not as accomplished a writer as her daughter. Mary Jane's formal learning undoubtedly took place in the common schools of Turner followed by informal learning at home.[3]

One major difference between mother and daughter was religion. Mary Jane's letters are singular for their pragmatism and lack of religious expression. She reflected on the difference between her and her mother when she told her daughter, Angie, that she did not attend church in San Francisco nor did she keep the Sabbath the way her parents did. Speaking of her mother, Mary Jane said, "I suppose she thinks I am very wicked but no one respects the pure religion more than myself which is to do as you would be done by." In Rebecca Cole's surviving note, she calls on God to bless the Megquiers and thanks God "for preserving their lives through so many dangers."[4] A family story partially explains Mary Jane's comment that although she loved her father, mother, and brother, Horace, she had "no love for the good town of Turner." The church elders, so the story goes, once called on the Coles to reprimand Mary Jane for attending a dance.[5]

When she was only eighteen, Mary Jane married Dr. Thomas L. Megquier, who was at least eleven years her elder. Thomas's grandfather was a pioneer farmer in New Gloucester, where Thomas was born, probably in 1801 or 1802. Thomas was well educated for his times. He attended Gorham Academy and received a medical degree from Bowdoin College in 1827. More than did Mary Jane, he constantly encouraged his children to go to school so they could prepare for the modern world. Four years after their marriage in 1831, the Megquiers moved to Winthrop where he practiced medicine until they left for California. Winthrop was a larger town than Turner and its economic base depended on textile and shoe manufacturing as well as farming.[6]

Like most diaries and collections of letters, the letters are discontinuous, and they end without a conclusion. Indeed, many readers of the first edition have wondered if Mary Jane Megquier settled in San Francisco or if she returned home. They may be surprised to learn that she moved back to Winthrop, Maine, even after she discovered that she preferred life in San Francisco where, she said, "The very air I breathe seems to be so very free."[7] By then a widow with friends, activities, and even a means of self support in San Francisco, Mary Jane Megquier returned to small-town life in Maine compelled by the desire to be close to her grandchildren and nearly grown children. The birth of a granddaughter and then a grandson made the separation from her family unbearable to her. She vainly tried to convince family members to join her, although she was not certain she wanted them to risk the journey. When her arguments failed, she completed her third round trip across Central America back to Winthrop. There she spent the rest of her life.[8]

Because the Megquier letters were written to her daughter, Angie, both before and after Angie's marriage to Charles A. Gilson, they are frank and straightforward. Mary Jane wrote to Angie as one would correspond with a sister and confidante more than as if she were writing to a daughter, reflecting the nineteen-year separation in their ages. Although Angie was only seventeen at the beginning of the Megquiers' journey and did not have the direct care of her younger brothers, it is clear that Mary Jane expected Angie, as the eldest child and daughter, to look out for the best interests of her brothers. John, at fifteen, was only two years younger than Angie, and Arthur, at nine, eight years younger, yet Mary Jane called them boys, even when John was twenty-two. She was full of maternal advice in her letters to them, advice noticeably missing in her letters to Angie.

The letters are especially valuable for their immediacy, sometimes describing events as they were actually happening. Her vivid writing reveals a sense of wonder and is full of the specific detail of a seasoned reporter. The dangers and physical discomforts of her journeys across the Isthmus of Panama and Nicaragua were endured without complaint and served to provide material for her stories. She described jiggers, land crabs, swarms of mosquitoes, an encounter with a nine-foot snake, and the slaughtering of a pig with equal equanimity. Everywhere she was impressed by the flowers and bird life. The letters are free from the literary pretention of women who traveled the same route and wrote expecting to be published or at least have their letters widely shared.[9] The level of her literacy compares favorably to her husband's even though he had the advantage of higher education.

The most significant journey in the letters of Mary Jane Megquier is neither her first journey across Panama nor the latter two across Nicaragua but her personal one, changing from being an adjunct to her husband to becoming an independent individual. Her letters provide another look at the issue of power between a husband and wife in making decisions that affect a whole family. Although Mary Jane was considerably younger than her husband, she does not show particular deference to him even in the beginning.[10]

In January 1849 Mary Jane's husband and his associates decided at the last minute that she should accompany him to San Francisco where he planned to practice medicine and open a drug store. The original plan was for Thomas to open a medical practice in the Sandwich Islands, but when news of the "gold excitement" reached them, the destination was quickly changed to the West Coast. Mary Jane agreed with her husband on the necessity of his trying his luck in the West, because, as he said, he "labored in Winthrop twelve years . . . day and night" with little compensation and accumulated debts. The surprise came when he decided that she should go along. The men were trying to be well prepared for their venture and as Mary Jane put it, were "going to take out an iron store and house, and they think some of taking me with them. It is so expensive getting women's work, they think it will pay well." She was willing to go and would "leave in good spirits," she said, "were it not for my children." The children were sent to live with members of the local Odd Fellows lodge and with relatives.[11]

She gamely sewed herself a tunic and trousers and her husband presented her with a sidesaddle for the mule ride from Chagres to Panama. She was the only woman among two hundred passengers on the steamship from New York to Chagres, and by the time she reached Panama, she began to see herself as an individual adventurer. "Women's help is so very scarce that I am in hopes to get a chance by hook or crook to pay my way," she told her daughter, adding, "a woman that can work will make more money than a man." After discussing the amount of gold men had already dug, she made a promise to her daughter couched in a metaphor that marked her difference: "In about one year you will see your Mother come trudging home with an apron full."[12]

Her independent point of view continued even when she reached a low ebb after landing in San Francisco. During the first summer she wrote about how hard she worked taking care of "a family of twelve" and said she would only stay "long enough to make a small pile of the dust." She quickly explained that she was not "sick of my bargain, not at all," because they had "made more money now than we could in two years at home." Her lack of news from home, however, gave her "a heavy heart."[13]

During the first winter and spring, Mary Jane entered the social whirl of San Francisco, describing dances, parties, and theatrical events, attending many of them without Thomas who was sick for a two-month period. She noted rather wryly that she would like to have Angie come but that Thomas disagreed. "I suppose," she explained, "he is afraid you will be led astray. He has his hands full to keep me straight." During one dance she "was engaged four dances ahead" and for a party at the St. Francis Hotel, she made a new "rose colored silk" beginning it one day in the late afternoon and finishing it the next.[14]

Mary Jane felt a new freedom because "there is no such thing as slander known in the country, no back biting, every ones neighbor is as good as himself." Yet still her children haunted her and made her "feel," she said, "as though I should fly when I think of the distance between us." Her anxiety about her children produced a dream that her younger son had drowned. The arrival of relatives and acquaintances from Maine helped her feel connected to family; she enjoyed both their company and their trials.[15]

Her new life-style contributed to her sense of self direction. When she ran the boarding house, which involved baking six loaves of bread and four pies a day on top of purchasing food, preparing meals, making beds, washing, and ironing, she turned out a prodigious amount of work. She commented that "if I had not the constitution of six horses, I should have been dead long ago." She clashed with the Chinese servant she hired to help in the kitchen. On her own she made hundreds of decisions every day.[16]

When the Megquiers returned to Maine for the first time, in the spring of 1851, they took the first step toward making a permanent home in Maine. Thomas bought the eighteen acres and a barn on Bramhalls Hill in Winthrop where they eventually built their large house. They stayed in Winthrop until Angie's marriage to Charles Gilson early in March 1852, but both returned because their San Francisco real estate investment was in jeopardy. When Thomas's partner unexpectedly died, they were forced to remain if they wanted to obtain a settlement.

It is during the period after their return from Maine that Mary Jane began to assert herself more strongly. Thomas complained more and more of headaches, but his affection for his family is revealed after the birth of their first granddaughter. She was born the day before Christmas 1852 in Portland, Maine, where the Gilsons were living. They named the child, Jennie, undoubtedly for Mary Jane, whose nickname was Jennie. Thomas Megquier wrote his daughter: "Our Jennie in Cal. would fly to Portland to kiss that very sweet little baby" and noted that when a neighbor called Jennie grandmother, "Jennie starts up & looks as young as a sweet eighteen." He also cautioned Angie to be careful of her health, explaining, "because your mother can endure so much, is no certain guarantee for you."[17]

Mary Jane continued to work at the many tasks connected with running a boarding house but developed a strong desire to return to Maine to see her new granddaughter and the rest of her family. A bout of homesickness in the early summer of 1853 brought her comment that everything is dry "while with you everything is beautiful." She continued, "I do want to see it and if I live, shall, another spring, whether your father comes or no." Mary Jane's connection with her daughter was so close that twice she noted that they wrote to each other on the same subject at the same time. Her desire to see her family impelled her to return to Winthrop by herself the following spring, leaving Thomas behind, his affairs still unsettled. He wrote to Angie that he expected Mary Jane to supervise the building of their house on Bramhalls Hill in Winthrop that summer. He contributed plans and probably returned in time to help. The substantial white house designed in Italian villa style with an attached barn was probably built in the summer and fall of 1854. Still a landmark, it sits high on a hill in Winthrop overlooking Lake Maranacook.[18]

It is not clear what happened to estrange Mary Jane from Thomas Megquier. When the estate of Thomas's partner was still not settled in 1855, Mary Jane decided to return to San Francisco for the third time in order to protect their investment. Thomas remained in Winthrop, probably unwell. She traveled via the Nicaraguan route with a young woman from Maine, named Emily, who was going to San Francisco to try to reunite with her husband.

Thomas died without a will not long after Mary Jane arrived in San Francisco. Before she learned about his death, Mary Jane wrote an unexplained, somewhat bitter letter to Angie saying, "I have never regretted for a moment that I left Winthrop. That beautiful house has no charms for me at present and should I know I would never visit it again, it would give me no sorrow as I should have the trials I have endured there." About her husband's illness, she said, "If he should be taken away, it will only be what I have wished that might come upon myself, rather than live with one who was ever wishing me to sacrifice my health to his gratification."[19]

She relented somewhat a few months later, relieved that Angie did not regard her as "an indifferent wife and Mother." She explained that she would return to Maine as soon as she could because she is "anxious to be square with the world, and place the boys above want." She noted, however, that if she must "work hard for a living," she would "rather do it here than home." Her valuation of self-support was underscored by her comments after the divorce of her companion, Emily, who had not succeeded in saving her marriage. Mary Jane was surprised when Emily kept her employment as a courtroom copier secret from her family and friends at home. She told Angie, "I thought it honorable in her to try to support herself."[20]

Now almost entirely on her own, Mary Jane wrote that she saw her home in Winthrop "as my final home." But this time it was she, not Thomas, who stated that she was not ready to return to Maine "until I can procure for my children the reasonable comforts of life without intruding upon any ones generosity but my own."[21]

That she valued her independence above all else was clear when she explained that although she had "an ardent wish" to be in "that beautiful house . . . nothing reconciles me but to look upon what I have suffered and should still unless I was independent." Despite the fact that she found a life that was "free and easy" in the West, her final decision was to return to Maine and the family claim.[22]

What caused Mary Jane Megquier's final outburst against her husband can only be surmised. While she may have felt used or taken for granted, the issue was undoubtedly money. The December after their house was built, Thomas Megquier took out a large mortgage on the house and land. The ownership was not cleared up until November 1856, a few months after Mary Jane returned from San Francisco for the last time. For a sum of money, the property was divided between Mary Jane, who was guaranteed a third of the interest in the property, or what would have been her dower right, and the children, who received the remaining two-thirds. Because Angie's husband, Charles Gilson, was a successful businessman, it can be assumed that he helped settle the mortgage.[23] In 1861 John and Arthur sold their interests to Mary Jane Megquier making her a joint owner with Angie Gilson.

Although the Megquiers did not make a fortune from the Gold Rush, they did realize enough money to build a prominent house and farm on a large piece of prime land that would be enjoyed by their direct descendants for nearly a century. The house was indeed Mary Jane Megquier's apron full of gold. But in addition to the Megquier's marital problems, the feat exacted other costs. Thomas Megquier lived only a year after the house was built. He died at the age of fifty-three, and he never met his goal of being debt free. The stress of the effort to propel his family into the modern world financially secure may have cost him his life.

On her part, Mary Jane Megquier had a taste of life in a freer society but gave it up to be with her family. She returned to a small town where she predicted she would have "many lonely hours" and be subject to small town gossip. Although she was sorely tempted, when none of her family would join her in San Francisco, she gave up "the frolic and dancing" she enjoyed so much, knowing that she would "miss them at home."[24] Little is known about Mary Jane Megquier's life in Winthrop after she returned from San Francisco, by then in her mid-forties, but it can be assumed that her children and grandchildren continued to be the focus of her life. Angie and Charles Gilson had six children. Although they continued to live in Portland until Charles died in 1880, Angie and the children spent summers with Mary Jane in the Megquier house they named "Beechcroft." One of the sons, Arthur Scott, became a doctor like his grandfather, and his son and namesake become a professor of medicine. After Charles Gilson's death, Angie and her unmarried daughter, Anne (Nan), lived year round in the Megquier house. Mary Jane died on December 9, 1899, two days before her eighty-sixth birthday. Shortly before her death she sold Beechcroft to Angie for one dollar. The house continued to be a center during the summer for the family, by then including great grandchildren, until 1938 when it was sold to Winifred Leavitt, a teacher in Winthrop. She passed down its story to the next owners when she left it in 1974.[25]

Although Mary Jane Megquier's story was always part of the Gilson family lore, her grandchildren thought her Gold Rush experiences should be shared with the wider world. Two Gilson daughters, Nan and Marjary Gilson Lund, transcribed the letters so carefully saved by Angie Gilson. Marjary, a librarian, who was a graduate of Smith College in 1902 and of the New York State Library School, moved to Arizona after her marriage. Shortly before the family sold Beechcroft, she placed the letters and the transcription in the Huntington Library, San Marino, California, where they, to this day, continue to be read by many researchers.[26]

FOUR GENERATIONS OF COLE WOMEN ABOUT 1856: FROM LEFT: MARY JANE MEGQUIER, REBECCA POLLARD COLE, JENNIE GILSON, ANGELINE MEGQUIER GILSON [1993].

I would like to thank the Huntington Library for allowing the publication of this new edition of the Megquier letters. A special acknowledgement is due to Arline Andrews Lovejoy, whose search of deeds and probate court and cemetery records led to the solution of the mystery of what happened to Mary Jane Megquier, to the location of the house on Bramhalls Hill, and to Mary Jane's great granddaughter, Anne Gilson Winslow. In turn, Anne Winslow willingly and helpfully shared the Megquier and Gilson family pictures, artifacts, genealogy, and stories that so enhance this new edition. Special thanks are also extended to her.

Robert Glass Cleland's useful footnotes and illustrations have been preserved. New footnotes and illustrations are followed by the notation: [1993]. The editing of the restored portions of the letters conforms with Cleland's style of making very few changes from the original letters, consisting mainly of ending particularly long sentences and beginning a few paragraphs. The new edition divides the letters into three sections, one for each journey.

March 1993

NOTES

1. Robert Glass Cleland, *Apron Full of Gold: The Letters of Mary Jane Megquier from San Francisco, 1849-1856* (San Marino, California: The Huntington Library, 1949), pp. v, viii.

2. For discussions of these issues see Susan Armitage, "Women and Men in Western History: A Stereotypical Vision," *Western Historical Quarterly* 26 (October 1985): 381-95; Elizabeth Jameson, "Women as Workers, Women as Civilizers: True Womanhood in the American West" in Susan Armitage and Elizabeth Jameson, eds., *The Women's West* (Norman: University of Oklahoma, 1987), pp. 145-64; Katherine G. Morrissey, "Engendering the West" in William Cronon, George Miles, and Jay Gitlin, eds., *Under an Open Sky: Rethinking America's Western Past* (New York: W.W. Norton, 1992), pp. 132-45.

3. Everett S. Stackpole, *History of Winthrop, Maine with Genealogical Notes* (Auburn, ME, 1925), p. 334; U.S. Census 1850, Androscoggin County, Turner, ME, p. 23; Rebecca Cole to Angie L. Gilson [hereafter cited as ALG], on back of Mary Jane Megquier [hereafter cited as MJM] to "My dear children," 15 May 1852, in the Megquier Collection, Huntington Library. The needlework is in the possession of Anne Gilson Winslow.

4. Rebecca Cole to ALG; MJM to Angie L. Megquier [hereafter cited as ALM], 30 June 1850.

5. MJM to ALG and Charles A. Gilson [hereafter cited as CAG], 12 July 1852; interview with Anne Gilson Winslow, 19 March 1993.

6. The information about Thomas L. Megquier's background used by Robert Glass Cleland was from George Thomas Little, *The Genealogical and Family History of the State of Maine* (New York: Lewis Historical Publishing Company, 1909), v. 2, pp. 624-25, and *General Catalogue of Bowdoin College and the Medical School of Maine, 1794-1950* (Brunswick, ME, 1950), p. 441. Little lists 1795 as Thomas's birthdate, but his gravestone in Winthrop and Bowdoin both give 1802. Conflicting evidence about his birth came from his granddaughter, Jennie Gilson Wilder, who, in 1930, said that Thomas Megquier's mother was a Merrill and because she died when he was born, Thomas was brought up by two maiden aunts in New Gloucester. The evidence points to the family's oral tradition as being the most likely as opposed to George Thomas Little's account. Thomas is not listed in the New Gloucester town records as one of the eight children born to William and Thankfull Haskell Megquier identified by Little as Thomas's parents. However, a Sarah Merrill married Edward C. Megquier in New Gloucester in 1789 and they lived in Poland. She died in 1801 leaving two children not named in the town records. John Megquier of Poland, who was born circa 1794, is the person who gave Thomas a mortgage settled in 1848. John, the son of William and Thankfull Megquier, identified by Little as Thomas's brother, died in 1840. It is most likely that the John who gave Thomas a mortgage was his brother and that the other John was a cousin.

POLLY WELTS KAUFMAN   XXIII

Marion Vose Gilson and Arthur Scott Gilson, Jr., "Ancestral Charts and Historical Notes" in possession of Anne Gilson Winslow; Virginia T. Merrill, *Merrill in America* (Solon, ME: V.T. Merrill, 1989), v. 2, p. 175; U.S. Census, 1850, Cumberland County, Poland, ME, p. 55; Thomas L. Megquier [hereafter cited as TLM] to John Megquier of Poland, ME, 28 November 1848, Book 163, pp. 108–10, Kennebec County Registry of Deeds, Augusta, ME.

7. MJM to ALG; 29 November 1855.

8. U. S. Census, 1860, Kennebec County, Winthrop, ME, p. 23; Gilson, "Ancestral Charts."

9. See in particular, Jessie Benton Fremont, *Year of American Travel* (New York: Harper and Brothers, 1878), pp. 4–67, 104-21, and Mallie Stafford, *The March of Empire Through Three Decades* (San Francisco: Geo. Spaulding & Co., 1884), pp. 8-63. For good summaries of women's journeys to California via Panama, see Glenda Riley, "Women on the Panama Trail to California, 1849-1869," *Pacific Historical Review* 55 (November 1986): 531-48 and Joann Levy, *They Saw the Elephant: Women in the California Gold Rush* (Hamden, Connecticut: Archon Books, 1990), pp. 30-52.

10. For discussions of husbands' control over family decisions about emigration to the West on the overland trail see John Mack Faragher, *Women and Men on the Overland Trail* (New Haven: Yale University Press, 1979), pp. 163-68, and Lillian Schlissel, *Women's Diaries of the Westward Journey* (New York: Schocken Books, 1982), pp. 10, 28, 30, 35.

11. TLM to J. Milton Benjamin, 14 January, 21 February 1849; MJM to ALM, 7 January 1849. In late November 1848, Thomas Megquier sold his house in Winthrop and settled the mortgage taken from John Megquier of Poland for a slight profit. TLM to John Megquier, 28 November 1848 and James Batchelder to TLM, 29 November 1848, Book 163, pp. 108-10, Kennebec County Registry of Deeds.

12. MJM to ALM, 24 February, 12 May 1849.

13. MJM to ALM, 29 September 1849.

14. MJM to ALM, 18 November 1849; 16 June 1850.

15. MJM to Rebecca Cole, 28 April, 1850; MJM to ALM, 14 August, 19 April 1850.

16. MJM to ALM, 30 June 1850.

17. TLM to CAG and ALG, 28 February 1853.

18. MJM to "My dear children" 31 March 1853; MJM to ALG, 15 May 1853; MJM to ALG and CAG, 15 June 1853; TLM to ALG, March 1854.

19. MJM to ALG, 29 November 1855.

20. MJM to ALG, 4 February 1856.

21. Ibid.

22. Ibid.; MJM to ALG, 19 June 1856.

23. Charles Gilson, U.S. Census, 1860, Cumberland County, Portland, ME, p. 25.

24. MJM to ALG, 19 June 1856. For a comparison with Mary Jane Megquier's experience running a boarding house in San Francisco in the same period, see Jerusha Merrill, "We are satisfied to dig our gold in San Francisco," in Ruth Moynihan, Susan Armitage, and Christiane Fischer Dichamp, eds., *So Much to Be Done: Women Settlers on the Mining and Ranching Frontier* (Lincoln: University of Nebraska Press, 1990), pp. 7-14.

25. Author interview with Anne Gilson Winslow, 26 March 1992; Rose O'Brien, "Winthrop's Apron Full of Gold House Has Romantic Background," *Lewiston Journal*, 27 July 1957;

MJM to ALG, 11 May 1899, Book 431, p. 356, Kennebec Country Registry of Deeds; letter to author from Jenifer McCullough (owner of house in 1992), 6 April 1992.

26. Interview with Anne Gilson Winslow; introduction to Megquier papers. Among the scholars who have used *Apron Full of Gold* in their works are: Julie Roy Jeffrey, *Frontier Women: The Trans-Mississippi West, 1840-1880* (New York: Hill and Wang, 1979), pp. 120, 126, 141-45; Schlissel, *Women's Diaries*, pp. 62-64; Levy, *They Saw the Elephant*, pp. 33-52, 142.

POLLY WELTS KAUFMAN

INTRODUCTION
TO THE FIRST EDITION

ROBERT GLASS CLELAND

The literature of the Gold Rush is amazing in its variety and volume. Hundreds of the Argonauts kept diaries of their expeditions by land and sea to California; many hundreds more wrote frequent letters to their relatives and friends back in "the States." These writings, whether journals or letters, naturally differ widely in historical and literary value; but nearly all throw some light upon the extraordinary conditions of the time and add details of greater or less significance to an episode that for sheer magnitude and drama had no counterpart in American life.

The following letters contain little of the melodrama of the Gold Rush but much of the substantial, commonplace stuff of the people's daily life; and if they lack the color and romance depicted in a California Centennial pageant, one may find in them some things of even greater interest—the reaction of two ordinary Americans from a restricted provincial background to a tumultuous, swashbuckling, unconventional society; the loneliness and heart-hunger caused by family separation and the long, futile wait for messages and letters; the remarkable interplay of the old and the new, the survival of culture and conventions in a life intolerant of restraint and a total stranger to tradition. Most of the letters were written from San Francisco, or en route to California, by Mary Jane Megquier, the wife of Dr. Thomas Lewis Megquier of Winthrop, Maine, and were addressed to her children, a few close relatives, and friends. The remainder were contributed by Dr. Megquier.

Dr. Megquier, the recipient of a medical diploma from Bowdoin College in 1827, was the grandson of a certain John Megquier whose tombstone in the churchyard of New Gloucester bore the following inscription:

Sacred to the memory of John Megquier. Died Dec. 27, 1825, aged 92. He was one of the proprietors and first settlers of New Gloucester and was one of those who felled trees on the spot where his remains are now deposited. A patriotic citizen and an honest man.

In 1831 Dr. Megquier married Mary Jane Cole of Turner, Maine. Four year later he moved to Winthrop, where he practiced with indifferent financial success until 1848. A family friend, then serving as United States Consul in the Sandwich Islands, finally persuaded him to leave Winthrop and open an office in connection with the consulate in Hawaii.

Megquier was planning to make this move when the gold excitement in California induced him to change his destination to San Francisco. For a time he expected to go alone to California, but the probable need for his wife's help and the high wages women were then receiving in San Francisco led to a change of plan. As a result, the Megquiers arranged to leave their children in the care of relatives or friends in Winthrop and undertake the California venture together.

The small group, of which the Megquiers were a part, elected to go by the much-talked-of Panama route. The letters give a vivid though unexaggerated description of the extreme discomforts and hardships experienced in crossing the Isthmus, the confusion among the hordes of immigrants waiting at Panama for passage up the coast, and the wretched, fearfully crowded accommodations on the steamer that finally took the homesick exiles on to San Francisco.

According to family tradition, Mrs. Megquier was the first American woman to cross the Isthmus, and certainly Dr. Megquier was one of the first American physicians to open an office in San Francisco. Before leaving New York, he and one of his associates shipped a portable frame building around the Horn. From the data at hand it appears that this structure was set up on Jackson Street, perhaps between Sansome and Montgomery streets, and used as a drug store, doctor's office, and family apartment. In time Mrs. Megquier opened a boarding house and added a considerable revenue to the substantial income derived from the doctor's practice and the drug store.

After spending some two years in San Francisco, the Megquiers returned to Maine for a visit; but in April, 1852, they sailed again, this time by way of Nicaragua, for California. The crossing, by means of the San Juan River and Lake Nicaragua, was as full of discomforts and hardships as the Panama route and seemingly offered even greater danger from cholera and yellow fever.

After a thoroughly uncomfortable voyage from Nicaragua, on a steamer named the "Pacific," Dr. and Mrs. Megquier reached San Francisco, the city of dust and eternal wind, as one of the letters described it, on May 13, 1852. Dr. Megquier immediately became involved in a dispute with a business associate over financial affairs, and the latter's unexpected death left the situation even more confused.

A few months later Mrs. Megquier opened another boarding house and drove herself night and day to keep it in successful operation. Sometime in 1854 the doctor's health became dangerously impaired and the Megquiers returned to Maine. Apparently some serious marital difficulty developed and Mrs. Megquier sailed for Nicaragua, without her husband, en route again to California. Late in October or early in November she reached what had finally become for her "the good city of San Francisco," from which she had no desire to return. Settling her husband's business affairs and running a small boarding house occupied most of her time, but she found some leisure for theaters, concerts, and a pleasant social life with intimate friends. Dr. Megquier died in Winthrop in 1855. Mrs. Megquier remained in California for a least another year and perhaps much longer.

The Megquier letters are especially valuable because, as already noted, they deal chiefly with the undramatic aspects of San Francisco society from the beginning to the end of the Gold Rush and describe the life of the ordinary citizen during that tumultuous and historic period. Mrs. Megquier's letters, which, as already stated, make up all but a small part of the collection, have an added value because they present the era of the Gold Rush from a feminine rather than a masculine point of view. In this respect they do for San Francisco what the famous letters of "Dame Shirley" did for the diggings and the mines.

Mary Jane Megquier described the scenes, incidents, and daily life of what was then the fastest growing and most exciting city on earth as a woman saw them and with a woman's power of observation and consideration for detail. Her letters are therefore intimate and human and portray with remarkable fidelity the social aspects of the times. This is especially true of her comments on the actors and artists who crowded the theaters and concert halls of San Francisco during the early and middle fifties. The astonishing Dr. D.G. Robinson, unexcelled for sheer popularity among the early theatrical entertainers in California, and his ever-adoring but often heart-broken wife, were members of Mrs. Megquier's boarding house—and she describes him without benefit of costume or make-up. She thought little of Catherine Sinclair as an actress, but had a great desire to see Lola Montez in her famous spider dance, the "Tarantella," which many people considered too vulgar for respectable ladies to attend. A relative, "Uncle Horace," who frequently visited the Megquiers, was Mr. Micawber in the flesh. One wonders how many of his kind found new splendor and magnificence for their dreams in the Golden Age of the fabulous city of which these letters speak!

The family pronounced the name Me-gweer'. The original spelling and punctuation have been altered only here and there. Trivial personal or family references that have no historical significance and add nothing to the value of the letters are omitted. The title is taken from Mrs. Megquier's laughing promise, in one of her family letters, to "come trudging home with an apron full" of gold.

January 1949

CHAPTER ONE

FIRST JOURNEY

From Maine to San Francisco via Panama
December 1848 to January 1851
Mary Jane Megquier and Thomas L. Megquier

TURNER [ME] DEC. 17, '48

Dear Friend Milton,[1]

Sunday night, lonesome as death, you cannot imagine, how much I feel the loss of your friendly calls and the contents of those capacious pockets of yours. I have been to church all day to please the Deacon,[2] but I think there is but few who would make so great a sacrifice to please, although I say it. I assure you the hours have passed slowly but still I do not regret the change that has been made. There is some comfort in feeling alone in the world, the hope of meeting some of my old friends again and a review of the pleasant hours I have enjoyed in their company. It was a time that will ever be remembered by me, when I left you and the rest of my good friends in Winthrop, and had I given way to my feeling, I should have deluged you all with tears, but I thought it best to keep them back for my own amusement when I am alone, and I find them very convenient occasionally.

---

1. J. Milton Benjamin (1823–1909) of Winthrop, ME, a brother in the Odd Fellows Lodge whose members supervised the Megquier children while their parents were first in California. [1993]

2. Deacon Nathan Cole (1786–1859) was Mary Jane Megquier's father. A farmer in Turner, he was elected Deacon in 1814 of the newly organized Baptist Church which held its first services in his barn. Rev. W.R. French, *History of Turner, Me., From its Settlement to 1886* (Portland: Hoyt, Fogg & Donham, 1887), p. 123. [1993]

I am very anxious to hear from you. I want to know how the new Dr succeeds. I am aware there are some that do not feel very friendly towards Dr M[egquier] because he left without settling, but I think he done the very best he could, and if he should succeed they will be amply repaid for all their kind feelings to him. I have not received but one line from the Doctor yet, but hope to have another soon and shall give you the contents forthwith.

You see by this, that I am at Turner but expect to return to Buckfield this week. Please to direct to that place until ordered otherwise.

Write very soon, and accept this from your

friend Jennie

N. YORK DEC. 25, '48

Ange, My daughter,[3]

The bearer is Mr. Adams, & you will readily see, I have not started from N. York yet. I intend writing you before I leave, heard by the way you were in Portland with Aunt & cousin Mary, hope it will be convenient for you to remain for some time, if so I shall feel easy about you. Before I forget it, write by the return of Mr. Adams, probably next week.

I have not had a line from your Mother yet, have not heard from any of my dear Children- be a good girl & write I have written three letters to your Mother- hope to see her in N. Y. Mr. Adams will tell you as near as I can when I start.

Give friend Adams a bite of lunch if needed.

Wish you all Merry Christmas.

Ange, give them all a kiss & my best regards & wishes. In haste from your Dear father

T.L. Megquier

---

3. Angeline Louise Megquier (1832–1926), the Megquier's eldest child, who would turn seventeen in January, 1849. Her brothers were John Otis Megquier (1834–1907), aged fifteen, and Arthur Selwyn Megquier (1840–91), aged nine. [1993]

Dear Daughter

I arrived safe Thursday morning. The snow had blocked up the road that I did not get into Boston in season for the five o'clock train. I stopped with Betty[4] that night—found her well in the city of notions. Found your Father well and all were very glad to see me. It is very uncertain when they will be ready to sail the[re] is so much to be done. Brinsmade and Cyrus are going to take out an iron store[5] and house and they think some of taking me with them, it is so expensive getting womens work they think it will pay well, but it is not decided, if so we shall send you money as soon as we can, and Mr. Calkins thinks it wont be more than four or six months and all I want you to do is to make yourself and the boys comfortable any where you please. Tell Charles[6] I forgot to settle my hack hire but I will make all right—I want you to go and see the boys soon—you must write—

Your Mother

Dear Daughter:

I received your line, & read it with great pleasure. It would be gratifying to be able to send you a handsome present, hope to be able to before many months, shall recollect your curiosities, I shall give you a full letter before I sail, you must go & see John and Arthur as soon as you can. I hardly think it possible for me to go to Maine before I sail. It would give me pleasure unspeakable to see you & the boys, I hope to see my daughter before many years and to be

---

4. Bettie L. Benjamin (1824–98), who later supervised John and Arthur Megquier and in 1856 married J. Milton Benjamin. Stackpole, *History of Winthrop*, p. 279. [1993]

5. Cyrus C. Richmond (1825–52), a druggist in Hallowell, was Thomas Megquier's partner in the San Francisco enterprise. His wife, Mary, did not go to San Francisco until later. Stackpole, *History of Winthrop*, p. 571. [1993]

6. Charles Haskell was a cousin of Thomas Megquier and was a grocer in Portland. He often served as the Megquier's agent. He was born in New Gloucester in 1823. U.S. Census for 1850, Portland, Cumberland County, p. 420. [1993]

better able to help you better than at present—the prospects under which I go appear to be very flattering.

Your Mother spoke to me about your present, you shall do the best I can. Say to Mary I feel greatly obliged for the line she wrote & shall expect her to write more in your other letter. Say to her I am under great obligation to her for her kind wishes & shall expect to have a pleasant word from her & hers at California. Give Aunt my best respects & say to her I hope to be able before long to compensate in some measure her kindness to you—my best respects & wishes to Oliver and his wife and say to Mr. [Charles] Haskell I hope some day to be able to reward him for his kindness to you.[7]

My love to all from your affectionate

Father T.L.M.

NEW YORK JAN 14, 49.

Dear Friend Milton

I received your kind letter and should have answered it ere this, had I not waited to write you something of my future destiny, which will be decided Tuesday at two o'clock, the Dr is very anxious for me to go with him, as it is very difficult to get any thing done in the way of womens help, I have decided to go if they can get a passage for me in the boat with them, which sails sometime between now and July next but there is an immense quantity of business to be done before the company will be ready, we are going to start fair, for the purpose of getting the gold after it is coined, not to dig. I think the prospect is very good but God only knows how it will end, were it not for my children I should leave in good spirits, those I shall commit to the care of our bretheren, the Odd

---

7. Angie often stayed with Mary, Aunt, and Oliver, Portland relatives living with Charles Haskell or next door in 1850. Aunt is probably Mrs. Mary T. Reynolds, aged 48 in 1850; Mary E. is Charles Haskell's wife; Oliver and Emily Reynolds, aged 23 and 22 respectively, lived next door. Charles Reynolds, aged 15, lived with the Haskells. Ibid. The Portland City Directory for 1850 lists Charles Haskell and Mrs. Mary T. Reynolds as living at 65 Free Street. [1993]

PORTABLE IRON HOUSES,

RUST PROOF.

THE GALVANIZED IRON HOUSES

CONSTRUCTED BY ME FOR CALIFORNIA,

HAVING met with so much approval, I am thus induced to call the attention of those going to California to an examination of them. The iron is grooved in such a manner that all parts of the house, roof, and sides, slide together, and a house 20 × 15 can be put up in less than a day. They are far cheaper than wood, are fire-proof, and much more comfortable than tents. A house of the above size can be shipped in two boxes, 9 feet long, 1 foot deep, and 2 feet wide, the freight on which would be about $18 to San Francisco. There will also be no trouble in removing from one part of the country to another, as the house can in a few hours be taken down and put up. They require no paint, *and will not rust*; while the surface being bright, the rays of the sun are reflected, so that they are much cooler than either tents or painted iron-houses. They can be made of any size that may be desired, varying in price, according to size and finish, from *One Hundred Dollars* and upwards.

Although more particularly calling the attention of parties going to California to these Houses, I would also bring them to the notice of those either residing in or trading with

SOUTH AMERICA AND THE WEST INDIES,

As being equally suitable to those climates. A specimen House of the above description can be seen by calling upon

PETER NAYLOR,
13 Stone Street, N.Y.

PORTABLE IRON
HOUSE, 1849.

Fellows hoping in a short time to remunerate them for all their kindnesses to us, I suppose John will be at your place in the spring. I hope you will keep an eye upon him, see that he is well treated, and he does what is right in his capacity, but I shall expect you in San Francisco by another year without fail where you shall share all the comforts we have to bestow with an unsparing hand, I wish you would come to New York, nothing would give me more pleasure than to see you once more this side of the globe.

I called to see Betty in Boston, found her very pleasantly situated, but rather sorry that her home was broken up in Winthrop, (poor girl), I pittied her and I sincerely hope that some day we shall all meet again and enjoy life better than ever.

We have a very pleasant family circle consisting of eight, all in high life, and we have gay times, but still I would like to see our good friends in Winthrop. I have been out but very little but there is every thing going on to instruct, and amuse, and I think you would not do better, than to come and spend a week, I shall expect a line from you very soon as I am anxious to know how you are getting on.

From your sincere friend Jennie

My dear friend Milton

Sir, I have obtained the privilege of writing a line in J's letter. I will just say I have spent some lonesome hours here from all my friends & family, but I am not discouraged yet. I hope to see the time I can interest you & the rest of my good friends at some future day & hope to be able. I shall expect to see you in Cal. before many years if we make it our residence there.

T.L.M.

Am much obliged for your line, give my best wishes to all our Odd Fellows

NEW YORK FEB 18, 49

Dear friend Milton

Yours of the sometime I forget when, reached us, I was heartily glad to hear you harping upon the old subject - it seemed like old times. When I found how much the ladies were appreciated in the far west, be assured I was ready to start, (not only for their help, but for their good influence upon society. What think of that?) You wish to know about our company, it consists of about ten, there is seven I think, of which Mr Brinsmade is head, who take out a large number of machines for working gold, from which they expect to realize a fortune, besides thousands of other articles of merchandize which will be needed in the gold diggins,[8] they have sent most of their traps round the Horn, they take a tent with all the fixings across with provision for a three month tour at the mines before the ships arrive, you must not believe half you hear for the stories are got up by those who are interested in any particular route, for instance, those who are fitting ships to go around Cape Horn, say it is very bad Crossing the Isthmus, those who are going to New Orleans say it is best to go by Vera Cruz, so goes the world, They are all going across except one who has gone round in one of the ships, we take the propeller Chesapeake next Saturday between the hours of twelve and three for Chagres, where we shall take a small steamer Orus go up the Chagres river thence mules back for twenty four miles, then the steamer California for San Francisco, it is a long route, and a dangerous one, but I have not regretted for one moment that we left your peaceful village, but I assure you it is painful to leave my children, and if there should any thing come upon them that would follow them through life and blast their happiness, it would be lain to my neglect. The Dr has gone to Connecticut to see the parents of his partner. He said he must write you but whether he did or not he would like to be remembered to all his friends, you brothers in particular. That bill if you get hand it to John or Ange. Sam W. took one against Rollins. I wish they would get if possible and hand to them.

If we reach our destination I shall write you and expect an answer forthwith. I should be most happy to hear from you again before leaving. You can tell and act accordingly. Love to all especially Sam.

Your most sincere friend
Jennie

---

8. Score of ingenious—and unworkable—gold mining machines, devices, and gadgets were sold to California-bound prospectors by enterprising companies in the East.

My dear friend & brother,[9]

Sir, the time has nearly arrived that we leave our native shores & sail for that land about which there has been & still is a great degree of excitement. Milton, you will recollect I began to start for this journey before the Gold excitement. I think I hear you ask what my feelings are now. I answer the same as when I first started, the hearing of gold there, does not excite me in the least, I was, & still am, determined If I live, to get some money & a competency. I do it for my families' sake. If I die in the cause it cannot be said I did not try. True, it [is] trying to leave my children behind, it cannot be avoided. I laboured in W[inthrop] twelve years, yes, day & night, where is my compensation? You say I have won many friends I acknowledge it, very many, & let me say they twine about my heart still & always will while it continues to pulsate, & you, Sir, are one & let me say here I wish to be remembered especially to all Brother Odd Fellows singly and separately. Say to George Carr (I hear he is quite low) he has my sincere wish & prayer he may recover his health & spirits once more. Say to him for me have good courage. I hope yet to see him in Cal.

You may have some curiosity to know what arrangements I have made since I have been here loafing, I have not been idle. We have formed a firm of three, have bought about $10,000 worth of drugs & other sailable goods & sent them around Cape Horn, together with a building 26 by 40, ready to put up, when it arrives in San Francisco. I now calculate to make my stand there & attend to my profession as usual, my future success I shall endeavour to inform you of. I have friends in N.Y. that are willing to do for me what I ask, if it is silver or gold, don't I feel grateful.

. . . Milton, you will excuse me for writing the above.[10] I do it thinking he might have made a muss about it. I heard he had and I was anxious for you to know the facts.

---

9. J. Milton Benjamin
10. Omitted is a long explanation by Thomas Megquier of how he believed he was cheated by a man in Winthrop. [1993]

Jennie writes you as you see. I suppose she writes you to have an eye to John as it is expected he will live near you for some time. Will you please to keep a fatherly eye over him, with Brother Burgess. Have an eye to his school, & confere with Noah if necessary.

Please be particular and write us concerning the children how they get along &c &c. We expect Angie will be in Lewiston the spring and summer terms, call & see her if you can let her be where she may—

We sail in the Steamer Chesapeak next saturday, the 24th—expect to start from panama the 15 of March expect to arrive in San Francisco the first or middle of April, & I shall probably write Burgess every stoping place on our journey— My Dear friend, believe your sincere friend & well wisher,

Thos. L. Megquier

NEW YORK FEB 24

Dear Daughter

I promised you a long letter but time will not admit of it, & we sail to day at four oclock, and there is so many things to do, and my head aches so bad, I hardly know what to do. There is a great responsibility resting upon you and I hope you will sustain it with honor to yourself and the rest of the family. You know what I would like therefore I will say nothing more.

When you go to Winthrop get those letters and burn them. I think they are in the card table. You take up the rest of that bill at Mrs Weeks and Mr Kelly has an account I left with him which is to be handed to you.

We are going in a small steamer to Chagres, where we shall change and take another up the Chagres river about 75 miles then we take mules for 24 miles, then there is a large steamer for San Francisco which will take about 30 days if we have good luck. I have made me a double gown of red calico a tunic and trousers for crossing the isthmus and a white plaid muslin and a blue muslin de laine polka, it is made like a boys monkey jacket, your Father has bought me a side saddle which I shall give to you when you come. Mr Calkins is going with us, if he likes he will send for his family, and it will be a good chance for you to come, it is very hard to leave you but I hope it is for the best.

Tell mother[11] I received her letter, we had got that book some time before. I suppose she will think it strange but it am a fact so I purchased one of another kind—am very much obliged, and shall answer it from Ca. I want you to write every month and direct to San Francisco, Ca and it will come direct. We shall write you from Panama. Your father is going to put in a line if he gets from the boat in time. Give my love to all the friends and be sure and write.

From your Mother

I had a present of some nice lace. I send you a piece for a collar gather it a very little into a straight binding. I want you to fold the boys' letters and direct . . .

{In T.L.M's hand}

We go in the Northerner instead of the Chesapeak. Start 1st of March, Capt. Thos. S. Budd, direct for Chagres.[12]

My daughter I have returned from Connecticut just in time to write one word, & that is to read your Mother's letter after & do as she wishes. I can add nothing, only to say I wish you to learn all you can & be a virtuous girl that you may be beloved by all, This from your Father

When you wish to direct a letter to us, seal it and put my name on it, put it into an envelope & direct it to R.D.W. Davis Esqr. New York, 21 Broad st.

CHAGRES. MARCH 13, 1849.

Dear Ange

You see by date that we have arrived at that dreadful place. The first day of March we sailed from N. Y. in the splendid steamship Northerner, we had a fine northeast storm for three days, we were

---

11. Rebecca Pollard Cole (1792–1882) of Turner. [1993]

12. The Megquiers' frequent change of date and ship represented the uncertainty and confusion that attended all sailings to California during the mad days of the Gold Rush.

THOMAS L. AND MARY JANE MEGQUIER, EARLY 1850S [1993].

obliged to go two or three hundred miles out of our course, which has made our journey some longer but since that, we have had a succession of the finest weather you ever knew. For four days I was sick that I did not enjoy much but since that I have been able to be on deck but not able to write on account of dizziness in my head, I cannot begin to tell you half but of one fact, I have enjoyed it much better than I expected, there is about two hundred gentlemen and I am the only lady and in that case I receive every attention. I have the captains saloon and plenty of company all to myself. I have not seen any of the wonders of the deep excepting a great quantity of flying fish, there has been a number of whales seen by those on board but the wheels frighten away before I could get a squint. I had the pleasure of viewing Cuba in the distance, that is all the land we have seen since we left until to day at 12 oclock there was a cry of land when we were all on our feet in an instant to rest our eyes once more on the land, at three we anchored off Chagres when three boats put out to inquire into our whereabouts, they told us that the steamboat Orus had gone up river with passengers from New Orleans would return tomorrow when we shall leave for Panama, report says that it is very healthy the whole route, and no trouble in getting across but the crowd of people on the other side is so great that tickets sold for one thousand dollars but the steamer Oregon and two sailing vessels had taken them off,[13] the California had not got to Panama from San Francisco the last accounts, but was expected daily.

We have got a fine company and I anticipate some fine times crossing the Isthmus, we have a fine lot of provisions and if we have to wait I shall go to housekeeping. I should like a girl about your size to help me. I think if you were here you would enjoy it finely, it is the most beautiful spot I ever saw, the shores are covered with a thick growth of trees and in front of us rises one of those old castles that we read of, it is built of dark gray stone with its walls and towers looking very much as I had anticipated, there are wrecks of vessels lying around, on the shore are any quantity of huts built as you will see by looking on your map, there is a great cry on deck some one has caught a fish but another says it is but two inches long, I think I wont run, there was a beautiful little bird caught on board ship to day, there is a gentleman on board who is going out to make a collection of birds who was sick for three or four days, he says that he shall remember us as your Father tended him and I am in hopes to send you some beautiful birds when our company returns in August

---

13. For an excellent summary of the Panama Route, see John Haskell Kemble, "The Panama Route to the Pacific, 1848–1869," *Pacific Historical Review*, March, 1938, pp. 1–13 [published as a book in 1943: John Haskell Kemble, *The Panama Route, 1848–1869*, (Berkeley: University of California Press).]. In 1849 the Pacific Mail Steamship Company, which had been incorporated April 12, 1848, operated the *California, Oregon,* and *Panama* between San Francisco and the Isthmus.

We are having a great time getting out our baggage, first one scolding then another, there is so [much] confusion I dont know what I am about, every one that passes says give my love to her, I want to see you and the boys very much. I dont dare think of the distance between us, I want you to write to Mother and the boys as soon as you receive this and give them all the particulars likewise to Mary and Betty don't neglect it, I would write but it is impossible at present, tell Johnny he must write me and give me all the news in W[inthrop], this letter I leave in the boat to be mailed in New York, The Captain is going across with us, I shall write again at Panama to send back by the Captain. Your Father wants to see you all very much, he has had as much as he could attend too, to take care of the sick, it is acknowledged he is the must useful man aboard.

Tell Arthur not to forget his Mother, give my love to all, shall write to Mother when I get settled, write as soon as you receive this, I do not know as you can read this, my hand shakes and the boat shakes, I can not read it myself,

Read this to Arthur and tell him to write two words in your letter.

From your absent Mother

PANAMA, MARCH 20,

Dear daughter

In my last I wrote you we had just arrived at Chagres, we lay there until the next day, when they got up steam and went to a bay about ten miles it being impossible to take the passengers from the place where we were, we there had a delightful view of the country. A number of the crew went on shore found some shells and cocoa nuts in abundance of which I received a good share, the next day being the 15, the little Orus came out and took us to the town of Chagres again, where most of the party went on shore and dined but my feet was swollen that I could not wear my shoes (caused by want of exercise and a warm climate). Of course I was obliged to stay where I was, but we were so near that I could distinguish persons on shore. They have an Astor House, and the Crescent City, little huts about twenty feet square. They are built by running poles into the ground and a very steep roof covered by a species of palm leaf all on the same plan.

After dinner we began our journey up the river which is the most delightful view in the world, the banks were covered to the waters edge with the most splendid trees covered with a thick foliage of leaves and flowers the most brilliant hues that could be imagined large trees the form of our maple covered with the most beautiful red flower, I thought of you but it was impossible to procure them. Could we have gone on shore, the ground is so covered with all sorts of vines so thickly interlaced that it is impossible to travel through it. This steamboat took us to a place in English called the twin sisters, a small place of about half dozen huts of the same as those at Chagres where we rested until the morning when your Father, Mr. Caulkin and myself were stowed into a little canoe about two feet wide and twenty feet long, with baggage enough to load a stout horse in our country, when we were propelled along by two natives, one in the bows with a pole, the other in the stern with a paddle. They will pole and paddle five hours without stopping to take breath most of them naked, or nothing but a bit of cloth about their loins, the perspiration pouring off them in torrents. Our first stopping place was at one of the many huts along on the river where we got a cup of miserable coffee with our biscuit, we made our breakfast, the pigs, hens, doves, ducks, dogs, cats were all around us ready to catch the smallest crumb that might fall, the poorest most miserable looking creatures, it seems impossible for life to exist in such famished skeletons, we did not stop again until we put up for the night which was the most romantic scene I ever beheld, there were a few of the boats arrived before us. We took our seats on the banks where we had a view of the boats as they come up, the moment they set foot on land they hoisted their tents fried their ham, made their coffee, after supper, slung their hammocks, and retired as comfortable as in their own homes, but our party thought they must have the natives cook them supper — we had duck, chicken eggs, fried plantain, it was very amusing I assure you to see us eat, not a chair or table excepting a very small one, neither knife, fork, nor spoon, and to eat soup with a jackknife is no small job, the lady of the house took her seat on the ground beside the pots and dished out, as we called, they gave us an india rubber bed, belonging to the party which they laid upon a place built up for the mistress of the house, and your Father retired but there were so many coming in to see us, that I did not sleep an hour. They would come and look at me as one of the greatest curiosities in the world, at four in the morning we started again, would that I had the power of writing what I saw and heard. The air was filled with the music of the birds, the chattering of the monkeys, parrots in any quantity, alligators lying on the banks too lazy to move unless you went very near them, at eleven we called for a cup of coffee at a place where we got a very little milk the first I had seen since I had left the Northerner although they have large droves of cattle it is seldom you can get a drop of milk, they are too indolent to milk it, let the calves have the whole. Although the finest soil in the world, not a vegetable have I seen since I left the boat, except plantain, it is not the season for fruit—I have seen oranges, and lemons, green but none that were good.

At three oclock we arrived at Gorgona the head of boat naviga-tion in the dry season, there was a scene for a painter, four hundred Americans encamped in and about the town, we took lodgings at the Hotel Francois, your Father and me had the parlor a small room in front with an outside door, not a window no floor, you can sit and see lizards running around as spry as crickets, we had two cot bedsteads without the least thing on them, not so much as a pillow which was every article of furniture in the room. I had a great number of callers, the natives would come and stand in the door and look at me with perfect astonishment. We arrived Saturday. Sunday we took a walk down on the bank of the river and called on some of our friends that came in the boat they treated us upon biscuit and smoked beef, it seemed like calling on old friends. There are about six hundred natives that get a living by transporting the Americans and their luggage across the isthmus.

Monday morning we mounted our mules and started for Panama over one of the roughest roads in the world, in some places the mules would have to step down like stepping out of a chair just room for the beast to put his feet, which if he should make a mistep, we should be tumbled down into a lagoon an hundred feet deep. We had two letters on the road left by some of our company who went before which made it very interesting, we found tents pitched beside the road, kept by Yankees who had started for California but as there was no chance of their getting there at present, are making money selling coffee, rice, and stewed beans to those who are passing, after a ride of eleven hours on the backs of the most tired and worn out animals you ever saw, the towers of Pan. rose up before us. In the evening as we were riding through, you could not help thinking of home, to see so much misery, every thing is going to ruin the most splendid cathedrals of which there are six, all tumbling to decay. There is one in front of our window where you will see those miserable wretches kneeling before the virgin Mary one of them kept his eye on me all the time he was there. We are in a large hotel we have a large room on the second floor two cots a table and two chairs washstand. The floor has never been washed since it was built which I suppose is about one hundred years. It is finished like our barn with the exception of the windows of which there is none, there is a large double door opens on to the verandah, but if you do not exercise you can keep very comfortable as respects heat, although within a short distance of the equator there is a cool breeze constantly blowing which makes it very comfortable.

I will now describe our party, first is P.A. Brinsmade who goes ahead in making arrangements, next in age is Mr Aldrich from New York [who] has been a great traveller in the south married about four weeks before he started of course has a great deal to say of his Jane, next is Mr Jackson of Virginia a fine man he too has a wife and eight children. Next is P.H. Cowen from Saratoga a great wit makes fun for all the party has a wife and one child a Mr. Vandervoort an old bach, from New York, steady and clever as you please, Mr. Cigenbrog, a young man of one of the first families in New York a perfect gentlemen, then, Mr. Calkin, your Father and myself, Cyrus [Richmond] and three young men they take out to work for them. Dr. Boynton professor of geology Mr. Bell, ornithologist, Mr. Fry, a gentleman collecting different specimens of fish, have attached themselves to our party, which makes it the largest of the season. I have not seen an American lady since I left New York but I have received every attention and enjoyed it finely, I have been very well all the time since I recovered from seasickness excepting a headache when exposed to the sun. Shall fill another sheet to send by Capt. Budd. Your Father will write you a word.

From your Mother

PANAMA MARCH 24

We are still at Panama, the Captain with whom we sailed from New York leaves tomorrow which severs the last link between this and the states for the present, which would make me feel sad if I would give way to my feelings, but there are many here who have been waiting for many weeks and there is no prospect of their getting away at present, having no tickets in the steamer, that our prospects seem quite fair, The British steamer arrived last night, the one we are to go in is expected hourly, it will probably stop ten days then we shall be twenty days going to San Francisco, I would like to give you a description of this place but I cannot, but one thing I can say, no one can have any idea of the misery there is in the world until they have seen some of these old towns where everything speaks of misery and decay, there are a few spanish families who go to mass every morning looking very neat and well dressed, they have long black hair braided, or curled, in their neck, no covering on their heads, wear light muslins, and lace shawls, their hands and feet are very small, but their faces are any thing but handsome. There are twelve churches dedicated to the twelve apostles at which they assemble on different mornings, they have music, the priest mumbling over something all the while which neither understand, in the afternoon, the priests gamble and enter into every species of vice, and disappation, but they keep the natives in complete subjection, so much so, that you can trust them with

ANGELINE, JOHN OTIS, AND ARTHUR SELWYN
MEGQUIER, EARLY 1850S [1993].

untold gold, but they are but very little above the brutes, will take
a trunk weighing two hundred on their backs and carry it over
a road equally as bad as it would be to take it over any of the
mountains in Oxford where there is no road, and carry it 24 miles
in two days eating nothing but what they can pick up, fruit, or a
little rice. I have often heard you say that you would like to live
where you could get fruit, I have seen many kinds but none that I
liked, excepting oranges, and pineapples, but I have not seen any
good bread, milk, no butter, cheese, pies, nor cake, we have beef,
and fowl, eggs rice, fish, and coffee, we rise at six and have a cup
of coffee, and a roll, at half past nine we have breakfast, at four we
dine, then nothing more until morning.

The last of our party arrived here last night from Gorgona,[14] they counted the dead horses on the road which amounted to fifty-two, a distance of 24 miles which we should think was quite too many, but the natives think nothing of it, they buy them for eight or ten dollars, feed them on the tops of sugar cane once a day, and they are the most miserable looking creatures in the world about as large as our two year old colts. I should like to have John, and Arthur have one they are so kind and gentle. I have in attempting to give you an idea of Panama been driven off the track by those miserable beasts. To return again the Hotel where we are, is the first after passing through the gate which is surmounted by a tower with a large bell of which there are a great number but not one but is cracked or missing a tongue, but it is all the same to them, they take a stone, and hammer away, all right, nothing is repaired, the buildings are all of stone, and brick mixed which are falling out of the walls leaving holes for the cats, dogs, rats which are trooping through our room every night but they take a bee line from one hole to another not stopping to make our acquaintance, the roofs are covered with tile, the exact of our large creampots cut into lengthwise, and laid the round side up, the blocks reach from one street to another with verandahs on both sides with doors leading onto them, I have not seen a pane of glass since I left the boat, the streets are all paved, and when you have seen one house you have seen the whole, all on the same plan, the city is surrounded by a wall in some places thirty feet high in others it is level with the ground, on the back verandah, in the yard, you will see a monkey, horse, dog, pigs, hens, and turkey buzzards, all eating out of one dish, off a short distance is [the] broad Pacific rolling in to the height of twenty feet, when the tide is out you can not come within five miles of the town, of course large vessels come no nearer at any time.

---

14. "Passengers landed at the little village of Chagres, at the mouth of the river of the same name, and were transported to Gorgona or Las Cruces, at the head of navigation in native dug-out canoes. At times, part of the river trip could be made in steamboats." Kemble, *The Panama Route,* p. 10.

News has just arrived that two sailing vessels are coming, if so they will be able to take off those who have been waiting so long for passage There is a number that are going back with Captain Budd today, and I presume you will hear a great many stories from those who return, but do not give yourself any trouble, for we have not suffered for any thing, and if we were rich, I should not grudge the expense at all if we did not make one cent, to see what we have seen, and heard, you will probably not hear from us again until we arrive at San Francisco, I want to see you very much indeed it seems as though I must at times, then I am obliged to take a look at something to turn my thoughts. When you receive this you must write to Betty and Mary, and read this to every one who would like to hear it, if you are not at Turner send it the first opportunity and see that Johnny comes in for a share. Tell Arthur the whole story and that his Mother thinks of him every hour Give me love to all tell them they are ever present.

Your Mother

PANAMA, MARCH 24, '49

Dear Daughter,

Your Mother has written you a long letter, giving you a good description of our journey so much better than I could. I shall not attempt any addition, but I must say that our journey from N.Y. to Panama has been most delightful. I have often thought of you Johny & Arthur. See them as often as you can, encourage & tell them from us to be good children that they may be beloved by all with whom [they] are associated. We are very anxious they attend closely to their books, we expect you will without our particular request—Ange, your age is such it is important that you should mingle with the best society & not change for any amusements whatever.

We shall write you after our arrival at San Francisco, & shall expect a letter from you every few weeks. You must write the boys often, give them good advice. Write all the news you can get from

Winthrop, Turner & Portland. Write Charles Haskell & Mary R.[15] Say to them that we will write them from California, give them our best respects—& all our friends—Ange with much respect from your Father.

{In M.J.M.'s hand}
Tell Horace [16] I shall bring him a Panama hat when I come home. I want you should write them or send them these letters, shall write them as soon as I get to my journeys end and to Mother likewise write as soon as you receive this.

EXTRACT FROM *THE NORWAY* [ME] *ADVERTISER*

FRIDAY, JUNE 1, 1849

From a letter of a Lady who left old Kennebec, in February last, in company with her Husband, for California, addressed to her Parents in this country, dated Panama, April 22nd.

The demand is so great, provisions are enormously high—flour $50. a barrel, codfish 25 cents per pound, ham 50, and other things in proportion. The Americans are pouring in from all parts of the States, notwithstanding they have been written to, that it is very difficult to get a passage. Their thirst for gold is such, they start without a ticket or the means of getting a passage in a sailing vessel when they arrive here. They will gamble, thinking to add to their little stock and lose their last dollar. There is supposed to be about two thousand Americans here; every nook and corner is filled; many of them I think would not be recognized by their friends; they let their hair and beards grow, wear a red shirt and a pair of overalls and a slouched hat, looking less like civilization than the natives.

---

15. Probably Aunt Mary Reynolds who lived with Charles Haskell. [1993]
16. Horace Cole (1811–85) was Mary Jane Megquier's brother and only living sibling. He was a farmer in Turner and married to Phebe Leavitt. Their daughter Frances was born in 1844. Town Records of Turner. [1993]

The Doctor and myself, with a number of our party, have been stopping at the island of Taboga, about nine miles from this place, for two weeks. We went down in a canoe, had a fine view of the islands, covered with the most beautiful trees and foliage, and birds in such quantities that the island seems alive with them—they are so tame that you can go very near them before they will start; pelicans may be seen standing around the shores in flocks so large, they look like a cloud when rising from the ground. We saw two large whales and large schools of porpoises; they jump out of the water showing themselves to good advantage being about four feet long and well proportioned; they follow the schools of smaller fishes and the birds hover over them to pick up the pieces. We boarded at one of the best houses on the island—a framed one, plastered with mud and sticks, costing $1500. They use the hardest kind of wood. The worms would destroy a house built of soft wood, in two years, working on the inside, until it is a perfect honeycomb. Half of the house had a chamber floor, where we slept in hammocks or on the floor, although the richest man on the island had nothing to sleep on except raw hides. Some of the party bought hammocks, others slept on the floor. We could lie and see lizards crawling in every direction; we killed two scorpions in our sleeping room; the Doctor was stung by one, being exceedingly painful for a few hours. Another insect which is rather troublesome, gets into your feet and lays its eggs. The Dr. and I have them in our toes—did not find it out until they had deposited their eggs in large quantities; the natives dug them out and put on the ashes of tobacco—nothing unpleasant in it, only the idea of having jiggers in your toes.

Another great curiosity was the land crabs; they inhabit the mountains, except coming to the seashore to spawn, beginning on Good Friday, when the island is covered with them; they do not travel in the day, but as soon as the sun sets, there is a perfect rush; they climb over every obstacle in their way, unless it is something they fear; they go up one side of a tree fifty feet high and down the other, when it is not a foot through; they travel over the houses, and when there are holes between poles, they fill up the ruts to the depth of a foot, where they do not find a chance to get out as easily as they get in. The house which we occupied had a window on the side next the mountain, entering through which, they cross the floor in a direct line for the shore; when they did not hit the window, they would come in under the eaves, following the poles overhead. We went onto the beach one night and drove them up in waves; the natives are very fond of them, eating none but the females.

We took our fixins one day for a little tramp, about two miles to a grove of mango trees, growing somewhat like our elms, only the branches at the extreme end reach to the ground, forming a most beautiful shade. We had taken our breakfast of boiled pigeons killed on the road, and coffee raised on the island, and cocoa-nut milk, and were taking a little rest, when some of the natives sprang up, saying, mucho malo, which, in our language, means *very bad,* when, looking up, we saw a snake coiling itself among the branches; one of the party shot him; he measured nine feet, about as large as my arm a little above the wrist. In the course of the day, another came down the tree very near us, but of a different species, not so large, which was very soon dispatched. The gentlemen took them to the village, to show what big things they had done.

There was about ten of us and it took six native women to cook two meals a day for us. They prepare nothing beforehand, not even to husk their corn, which they do at every meal, then pound it in a large mortar until the hull is off, then they boil it, and mash it up and bake it on a flat pan, which was all the bread we had; they have no flour. They very often killed a pig for our breakfast. They tie all four of the legs together a process which the pig submits to very readily, hack his throat awhile with a large knife, they use for all purposes, something like your stoutest bush scythe, only not so pointed at the end (by the way, it is the only weapon they have, either for use or defense), then they scald him enough to start a few bristles, then skin and cut him into small strips, all on the ground where he is first killed.

Their beef they bring from some of the islands in canoes; when they land them, they have a long rope around their horns, the native takes the end around a tree, and draws it up gradually until he gets his head snug to the tree until it is fast, then he creeps up slyly and cuts his hamstrings, bringing him down behind, then giving him a cut on the back of his neck, he succeeds in cutting his throat, when he skins and cuts him up without moving him from the spot where he first falls.

Dear Daughter

Here we are yet in this miserable old town with about 2,000 Americans all anxiously waiting for a passage to the gold regions, When I wrote the last letter I think, there were no large vessels, and there did not seem to be any prospect of any, but they are coming in now every day, and taking the passengers off, but they continue to pour in from the states so there does not seem to be any less here, There are now two steamboats here but neither of them the one that we claim but we have heard from her and she is expected every hour, if she does not come, there is some prospect of our going in one of these, but shall be crowded tremendously, One of them is the Oregon which has made one trip to San Francisco and brings great news from there, the passengers that come in her, are all loaded with gold, but they have to endure many hardships, and it is almost impossible to get a shelter for your head, but womens help is so very scarce that I am in hopes to get a chance by hook or crook to pay my way, but some women that have gone there are coming home because they can get no servants to wait on them, but a woman that can work will make more money than a man, and I think now that I shall do that which will bring in the most change, for the quicker the money is made the sooner we shall meet, but I am very glad you are not here, although at times it seems that I must see you, but it would be still harder to see you suffer for the comforts of life. I am not at all concerned for myself as I can endure almost any thing and enjoy it, as is the case here, some think it is hard fare, but I am getting fat, with but two meals a day no flour cooked in any way except in sour hard bread, no butter have I seen since I left the steamboat, nor vegetables of any kind excepting beans without any pork, and a very few Lima potatoes for which we have to pay 18. dollars a week, but your Father has done nearly business enough to pay his expenses since we have been here, I assure you there is some fun getting two dollars a visit if you have to pay it away again, there is a great many sick and quite a number have died but your Father has not lost a patient, he took one from another physician which they said must die, and tended him about ten days for which he got fifty dollars, at that time he started for home in New York, They tell us our expenses will be as high again in S.F. not on account of scarcity of provision but of help, every body is digging gold, even the cabin boy has his thousands, they get in big lumps, one passed through this place weighing thirty six ounces pure gold. What think of that? in about one year you will see your Mother come trudging home with an apron full, but without joking, gold is very plenty and if I do not like we shall get it as fast as possible and start for home, they find some of the most precious stones. I saw a ruby that I presume was worth thousands of dollars, the gentleman told me he should present it to the college at New Haven.

The California mail was opened the other day. I was disappointed in not hearing one word from you, I hope you will not neglect writing once a month, as you must know that I want to hear from you and the boys very much. I was walking out the other day and saw a beautiful child, she put out her hand, I asked her Mother to give her to me, she said I could have her for one hundred dollars, if I had been on my return with as much money as those that are returning, I should have taken her, it is the only thing I have seen in Panama that I wanted, you could not help loving her, they seem to be very pleasant in disposition and some are quite good looking but most of them are most intolerably ugly.

About two weeks ago a sailing vessel came in from Callao,[17] she had been whaling but hearing of the excitement she went into Callao disposed of her oil and came here for passengers, she was

---

17. The port of Lima, one of the best known ports on the West Coast.

commanded by Capt Gardiner from Nantucket, his wife was with him, they put up here but they were so full we all slept in one room of course got pretty well acquainted, we had a great idea of selling our tickets and going with them, we went on board and sailed down to the island to get water, spent one day and on our return was becalmed, was obliged to drop anchor to prevent drifting with the tide, while we were there rolling lazily from one side to the other, the long looked for steamboat hove in sight, then we thought it best to go in the steamboat but it was not the one we expected and she is full of passengers but she says the California is coming to day. Capt Gardiner says Louisa's husband put into Payton a few weeks since for fresh provisions and water for another years cruise won't Louisa be disappointed she expected him home in March. He has done very well.

I changed my room when I returned, the one I now occupy fronts a plaza or common, on the opposite side are yankees, they have a cooking stove you can see them stirring up the good things, gentlemen I presume that never was in a kitchen have to sweat over that old stove about two thirds of the time to keep soul and body together, it comes rather hard but they submit with a very good grace, I wish you could see my bouquet of flowers, they are entirely different from any thing you see in the states, in the middle is a white flower with six long leaves around the stem, a bell shaped flower in the middle with seven long green stamens from out the very edge of the flower, it is so fragrant it fills the whole room, then there are two bunches something like our roses, there is about fifty buds and flowers on each, there is one some thing like our holyhocks which a gentleman has variegated for me then orange flowers which makes a beautiful bouquet and it is the only thing like civilized life in the room. The rainy season has commenced and the mosquitoes are so thick that it is impossible to sleep, last night we had a net and we got along nice.

May 20. Mr. Calkin received a line from home. By that I learned you was at Norway. I hope you will gain friends wherever you are and be happy. Say to your uncle and Aunt our prospects are flattering.[18] They shall be well paid for all their kindness to you. The first money we get will be devoted to your comfort and the boys. The most of our party have gone in the Panama, we expect to go in the Oregon, on Wednesday. I have formed a great many very pleasant acquaintances but they have nearly all gone and left us that we are quite lonely, I have seen a couple of young spaniards, a number of times. I shewed him your picture, he said, bonito which means pretty, I think if you were here you could make a bargain with him, you would have nothing to do but go to mass, a slave to carry a mat for you to kneel upon, and swing in your hammock the remainder of the day, he is very pretty and dresses in good taste, if he could talk English I would tell him to wait two years, and I would take him to the states. I suppose you have received the birds, you must keep them nice until I come when I will get them set up which will make them very pretty.

Give my love to the family. Say to the girls they must write. I hope you read Father's letter before sending it, if you received it first. We start this morning at ten, they say the California is coming in, if so all right. Your Father sends his love to all and lots to you and the boys, so adieu until I write from California. Mrs. Frederic Ilsley is sitting on the cot beside me from Portland. She expects to go home soon if her husband does not go to Cal. and will call and see Aunt's family.[19] She is in hopes to see you. She will give you all the particulars. Tell Aunt P[amelia] I should like to have her here for a few hours. We should have lots of fun there is so much to amuse one but it wont do to put it on paper. Write the boys and send them the line I have written.

your Mother

---

18. Horatio Cole, married to Pamelia, was a brother to Mary Jane Megquier's father. Their son was "Uncle Horace," who also came to San Francisco in 1849, probably called "Uncle" to distinguish him from Mary Jane's brother, Horace. William B. Lapham, *History of Norway Maine* (1886), p. 483. [1993]

19. Frederick Ilsley was listed as a shipmaster in California in the 1850 Portland City Directory. Aunt is probably Mary Reynolds in Portland. [1993]

PANAMA, MAY 14, 49.

Dear friend Milton[20]

Thinking you might like to hear of our whereabouts, I will try and rub open my eyes, and tell you some of our journeyings but it is an effort, the climate is such, that I cannot keep the day of the week, But to our journey, We started from New York the first day of March, after a very pleasant passage of twelve days we landed at Chagres a small village of about six hundred inhabitants living in huts built of bamboo poles supported by pieces of timber and covered with grass and palm leaves, At the left as you enter the harbor is a fine old castle built of stone by the buccaniers, it commands the whole harbor, it is surrounded by a moat, and a high wall on which you can see the guns peeping at you, many have fallen from their places, others will keep theirs for years to come, a negro is the only tenant. I think he is getting rich by charging one rial for admission, the Americans all rush to it in a perfect frenzy, it very soon abates after living in Panama a while. As you pass along the village you will see the Astor House still farther the Crescent City Hotel, where you get beef and fish by the yard stewed Monkeys and Iguanoes but my appetite has not been quite sharp enough to relish those yet.

The natives are cleanly in their person, and dress, they are a simple inoffensive people but understand perfectly, the getting of the dimes from the Americans. After stopping a few hours we started on the steamboat Orus with about thirty canoes attached to the stern filled with half naked negroes to take us to Gorgona from the head of steamboat navigation which in the dry season is only sixteen miles, to a small village called the twin sisters where we spent the night, it was a rich scene to see one hundred and fifty Americans crowded on to a boat the size of the celebrated Phoenix some trying to get a cup of coffee, others a change to lie but at last we got a chance to rest us for a couple of hours, when all was bustle

---

20. Mary Jane Megquier also described the journey in her March 20 letter to Angie, but many of the details are different. [1993]

and confusion again in making preparation for our journey up the river, our breakfast a cup of miserable coffee and hard bread.

After waiting three or four hours we were stowed into a canoe (Mr Calkin, Dr and myself) twenty feet long two feet wide with all our luggage which brought the top of the canoe very near the waters edge. We seated ourselves on our carpet bags on the bottom of the boat, if we attempted to alter our position we were sure to get wet feet, notwithstanding our close quarters the scenery was so delightful the banks covered with the most beautiful shrubery and flowers, trees as large as our maple covered with flowers of every colour and hue, birds of all descriptions filled the air with music while the monkeys alligators and other animals varied the scene, that we were not conscious of fatigue, Two natives pushed the boat with poles unless the water was too swift for them they would step out very deliberately and pull us along, Was it not a scene for a painter to see us tugged along by two miserable natives. There are ranchos every few miles where you can get a cup of miserable muddy coffee with hard bread of which we made dinner, then we doubled ourselves in as small compass as possible and started, under a broiling sun the thermometer at one hundred. arrived at our destination for the night about five oclock where we seated ourselves on the bank to watch the arrival of the canoes, before dark there were one hundred Americans on that small spot of ground all busy as bees making preparation for the night. Our party thought it best to have the natives cook their supper, it was rich to see us eating soup with our fingers, as knives, forks, spoons tables, chairs are among the things unknown, they have no floors, the pigs, dogs, cats ducks, hens, are all around your feet ready to catch the smallest crumb that may chance to fall, As I was the only lady in the party they gave me a chance in their hut but a white lady was such a rare sight they were coming in to see me until we found we could get no sleep, we got up and spent the remainder of the night in open air, At four we took up our bed and walked, Would to God I could describe the scene. The birds singing monkeys screeching the Americans laughing and joking the natives grunting as they pushed us along through the rapids was enough to drive one mad with delight. when we got tired sitting, we would jump out and walk to cut off the crooks which were many, we could never see more than ten rods, sometimes we would find that we were going northeast when our proper course was directly opposite.

At four in the evening we reached Gorgona, another miserable town, where you will find the French, New York, and California Hotels but you cannot get decent food, nor a bed to lie upon at either house. There is a church in town which is not as respectable as the meanest barn you have in town, they have the ruin of a bell, the tongue of another, hung three feet from the ground, with the addition of a drum made by drawing a bit of hide over the ends of a small keg which the little negroes use to good advantage in calling the congregation together, they divide it off with raw hides to prevent being overrun with domestic animals in time of service, a mule took the liberty to depart this life within its walls while we were there, which was looked upon by the natives of no consequence.

After spending two nights and a day at Gorgona we resumed our journey for Panama on the backs of the most miserable apologies for horse flesh that you could conceive off, they were completely exhausted carrying heavy loads over one of the roughest road in the world, nothing but a path wide enough for the feet of the mule, which if he should make a misstep you would go to parts unknown, many places so narrow it would be impossible to pass each other on horse back, the muleteer would give the alarm that they might stop on the opposite side. On the top of one of those high hills we found a nephew of Ben. Joys dishing out beans coffee and pancakes in a comfortable way, as there was no way of getting to Cal. he thought he [would] make a little money where he was. At five in the evening the towers of Panama showed themselves in the distance. I assure you they were hailed with joy after a fatiguing ride of 24 miles. Panama is an old spanish town, the house built of stone white-washed outside the roofs covered with tile, on the first floor a large entrance where you ride to the foot of the stairs which takes you to the second story where there are large doors opening onto a veran-dah from every room, they have no windows or chimnies cook on a platform built for the purpose, at the Hotel where we are, it is in the third story the smoke blows where it pleases. There are a great number of churches each having quite a number of bells which they contrive to keep some one thumping most of the time, in the inside you will see some of the good folks of olden time dressed in gaudy silks and satins but the most conspicuous is the virgin Mary holding the little Jesus covered with dirty laces and some splendid diamonds peeping out from among the cobwebs, candlesticks and a great many ornaments of silver but as it is not the order to clean, or repair you would not know of what they were made unless you were told, The town is surrounded by a wall twenty feet high and as many feet thick, on the water side it is surmounted by enormous big guns weighing two or three tons which the Americans have worn quite smooth sitting astride them looking for the steamer. . . .[21]

It used to make my blood chill when I read of our soldiers in the Mexican war finding scorpions in their boots but I have learned by experience that it is a trifling affair, besides I have had jiggers in my feet a small insect that lays its eggs in your flesh but all these things are nothing when you get used to them.

MAY. 20.

When we arrived here we did not expect to stay but a short time for want of coal the steamers have been detained until two weeks ago the Panama, and Oregon, arrived, one from Cal. the other around the Horn, the passengers [have] been pouring in from the states all the while until the town was overrun but a great number of sailing vessels have been in, and taken them nearly all, If it were not for the uncertainty which is hanging around us, I should enjoyed it very well I assure you, there is a great deal of excitement which you are well aware I enjoy, the Dr has done nearly business enough to pay our expense which is $18. per week, there is some fun taking the dimes if you have to pay them out directly. The news

---

21. A repetition of the story about the trip to the island of Taboga included in the extract from *The Norway Advertiser* is eliminated here. [1993]

from the gold regions far exceeds our expectations, every man that goes to the mines picks up a fortune. I have had a lump of pure gold, weighing two pounds in my hand, just as it was dug, as ladies are very scarce I expect to make money in the way of odd jobs such as cooking and attending the sick. We expect to take passage on the steamship Oregon, if nothing prevents will sail on Wednesday next.[22] I send this by one of our party who married a short time before he left, being detained so long he must return and see his fair one, I want to hear from you, and all our friends Remember me to them. Tell them if we succeed we shall give them a call in two years, some have made a fortune in three months. If John is with you in Winthrop see that he is comfortable read him this if you please and tell him I have written him in Angie's letter. Love to all and a good share to yourself. Write to S.F.

Your friend Jenny

Being detained here so long, the post master got leave to open the California mail, judge of our disappointment not one word for us. I hope I shall have no cause to complain in future. write all the news. Say to our friends shall answer all the letters I receive.

PANAMA, MAY 22, 1849

Dear Johnny

We are just starting for California. I hear that you do not want to go, after I have been there and write home what a nice place it is, you wont feel so bad; little boys of your age can make their hundred dollars per month. You need not give yourself any uneasiness about our being injured in any way, any more than in Winthrop and there is a fair prospect of your Father making money

---

22. Jessie Benton Fremont was also waiting in Panama for a steamer in May 1849. George Thomas Little states that Mary Jane Megquier entertained Fremont in her tent. Fremont sailed on the *Panama*, the other steamer that arrived at the same time. Jessie Benton Fremont, *Year of American Travel*, pp. 58–60; Little, *Genealogical and Family History of Maine*, p. 625. [1993]

enough in a year or two so we can come home. I want you should be a very good boy, that you will not be afraid to write your Mother all your troubles and pleasures. We have been here two months but your Father carries away more money than he brought besides paying twenty dollars per week for board. I suppose you will see all my letters of course I shant have to tell you of our journey. I have sent some birds for you which must be kept very nice until I come home when I shall get them set up, give my love to all the folks in Winthrop and write me a long letter tell me all the news. [I] shall write as soon as I get to San Francisco, be a good boy and write me a long letter,

From your Mother

Dear Arthur

I am now writing the last letter to my little boy that I shall write in Panama, I am going aboard the steamboat Oregon in the morning to go to California, then I will write you when we shall be ready for you, if there is no chance, I shall pick up the lumps and come home as quick as possible. I hope you will be a very good boy and do all for your Uncle and Aunt that you can. You must go over and tell Grandmother that your Mother is on the way again. Be sure and learn to write so as to make some scratches in your cousins letter. I want to see you very much. Give my love to the family and to Mr. P.

Your mother

John & Arthur, My Dear Children, your affectionate Mother has written you & given good advice, read it often & obey. I am very anxious for you to be good boys so that your friends all around you will love & respect you, pay good attention to your books, learn to read, write & spell & cypher well, let us be well pleased when we return & see you, be kind to each other & your mates & be obedient to those with whom you live. Always be attentive to meeting on the Sabbath. This I wish of you all three, John & Arthur, be good

This from your Father

Dear Daughter

I wrote you from Panama when we were to start for this place, which we did according to our expectations. At three oclock we went aboard raining as fast as it could pour, found about four hundred passengers five ladies and two servants.[23] Your Father visited a gentlemen in Panama who was sick with the fever, he has a wife and child, from Missouri. I was introduced to them first, and found them very pleasant indeed, Major Sewall and family and a Mrs Blanchard who expected to meet her husband in Cal. For the first two days I was quite seasick but I did not suffer so much from that, as from the heat, for the first two weeks I came near being roasted alive, after that it was impossible to keep warm, the gentlemen put on two overcoats and then they were as blue as pigeons. The first port we put into was Acapulco a small Spanish town situated on a most beautiful bay,[24] to look upon it from the ship it seemed the dwelling of the fairies but to go on shore it was the same as all other towns on the coast, very much dillapidated, the next stopping place was San Blas, where we had to coal and water which occupied three days. I did not go ashore it made me sick to get into their little boats so the ladies kept the ship. Your Father went ashore a number of times, he was perfectly delighted looking at the ruins of former magnificence, but the musquitoes and sand flies were so thick they were glad to get aboard ship, Our next port was San Diego where we left the party who are to run the boundary between this country and Mexico but they run away to the mines as soon as they are landed and leave Uncle Sam to look out for some one else to do his business, Our last stopping place was at Monterey eight miles below this a very pretty place, there I saw the first chimney in a house I have seen since I left New York.

---

23. The Megquiers sailed on the *Oregon*. On a previous voyage, the *California*, built to carry a maximum of 250 passengers, sailed from Panama with 365 persons aboard. The normal voyage during these early years required from 18 to 21 days. By 1853 the time had been reduced to ten days or two weeks. Kemble, *The Panama Route* pp. 8, 11.

24. The port of the Manila Galleon during the greater part of Spanish rule.

On Wednesday the thirteenth of June we arrived at this place which made three weeks we were on our passage, had it not been for the heat I should have enjoyed it quite well but you must bless your stars that you are not here at present, report says there are six thousand people here that have no shelter, but some are going and coming from the mines, so we got a small room the size of my bed room in Winthrop for five of us with our luggage, your Father and me lie on a single mattress on the floor one small pillow. Col. Hagen, wife, and little girl lie on a hard mattress on the bedstead, we have no fire, the weather is about the same as our cold days in April when the wind blows enough to take your head off, so we set here all huddled together, so cold we cannot sew, the wind blows all summer, the winter is the most pleasant part of the year, so says report. At the rate we have to pay for board it amounts to about four thousand dollars a year, some kinds of provision are cheap as in the states such as beef pork flour, but vegetables are enormously high, onions seven cents apiece pine apples sold for eight dollars apiece, potatoes shilling per pound, butter dollar and a quarter per pound. We have been here three days and have had nothing to eat but beef, pickled fish and poor flour bread. What think of that? If I could only get a house to live in I should make money but one boarding house rents for eighty thousand dollars a year, rent and labour is the reason board is so high, money is plenty as dirt if you have any means of getting hold of it, but we have not been here long enough to tell whether we can make any thing or not, but if your Father can get practice there will be no doubt but we can get money enough in a year or two to come home, there is seven millions of gold dust in this little place besides thousands of coined money, some that came on in the boat with us have made a fortune in speculations while others have been ruined. It is very unhealthy in the mines, thermometer in the morning at forty, at ten, one hundred and ten, put an egg in the sand it will cook about as quick as in boiling water, our party have all started for the mines to day which makes it quite lonely, if they should think it best your Father will go but we cannot tell what will be for the best.

I wish I could describe the town to you that you could have some idea of how we are situated but it is impossible, houses are going up in every corner but land is enormously high. Mr Richmond has got the refusal of a lot for six months for eight thousand dollars and if his building gets here safe he will make a fortune, they put up a few joists and cover it over with cotton cloth, make the partitions of calico which sell for nothing almost, many bring out goods but can find no place to put them, are obliged to sell them at auction for half what they gave for them in the states, the town has grown one half in two months but you must try and make yourself as happy as you can for present. I am in hopes by the next steamer to send you something but I hope you will write me by every steamer, not one word have I heard from you since I left. If I do not hear by the next steamer, I shall be very much vexed with you. Send this to the boys. I want to see you so much at times that it seems I should fly away but I am very glad you did not come, it is so expensive I am afraid we should suffer for a shelter. I think I wrote you that John Q. Cole[25] started from Panama, the day we arrived there, in a sailing vessel, he has been all this time getting here, arrived yesterday. He says Uncle Horace[26] left here yesterday for the mines. I was very sorry I could not see him but I shall probably hear of him at the mines. Give my best love to all your friends and mine and write all the particulars and all about the boys. I shall write you again by the next boat and if I don't have letters I shall not write any more.

From your Mother

My Dear Children

Your Mother & Father have been blessed with good health and spirits ever since we started, our whole object is to get something

---

25. John Quincy Cole, aged twenty three in 1849, was Mary Jane Megquier's first cousin, the son of her father's brother, Hiram of Lowell, MA. Stackpole, *History of Winthrop*, p. 334. [1993]

26. Horace Cole, aged nineteen in 1849, was also her first cousin, the son of Horatio and Pamelia Cole of Norway. Lapham, *History of Norway*, p. 483. [1993]

to make us comfortable, either here, or in the states, & we are anxious for you to be industrious, & spend all possible time in study. You must suppose we are anxious to hear from you. Six months have passed & not one word, you must write every month without fail & give us all the news send this to John and Arthur. My sons it is your Father & Mothers wish for you to be obedient & honest children & spend all your time in school closely to your books, & you never will regret if you spend all your leisure moments reading some historical or good books. Money is plenty here. I saw [a] small ordinary wire cage with one canary in it, sold for $20.00. Angie, if you are in Norway give Aunt and Uncle our best respects. Arthur, give Grandfather & Mother our best wishes & Uncle John & Aunt Sally[27] & Elizabeth &c. John, give the Winthrop friends our best compliments & ask them to write

Your Father

[SEPT. 1849?]

Very dear Cousin and Daughter

It is now very late, the mail closes tomorrow. It is with a heavy heart I write you, it being now seven long months since I have heard one word from Maine, excepting yours which gave no particulars of my children but was very glad to hear of the happy change you have taken upon yourself. As for giving you a description of my situation and those around me, it is impossible, it is a complete farce, a change comes over one, that you can with difficulty recognize your intimate friends, the greatest dandies wear their beard long, their hair uncombed, a very dirty colored shirt, and coarse jacket, their skin brown from the sun and dust; some collecting dirty clothes for washing, others driving a mule and cart for which they get their two ounces per day. Professor Shepard from one of the first institutions in the states is driving a cart from Sacramento

---

27. John, another one of her father's brothers, and Sarah Cole of Turner. Stackpole, *History of Winthrop*, p. 334. [1993]

city to the mines, from which he is coining a mint of money, every one must do something, it matters but very little what it is, if they stick to it, they are bound to make money. It is said there must be a general burst up here soon but I hope we shall sell first, Our building arrived two weeks ago. Richmond says if it was done he could take twenty five thousand for it, you may think that a big sum but there are many not as good as that rent for thirty thousand a year, people seem to be very near crazy. God only knows where it will end, some days we have made fifty dollars but I have to work mighty hard, a family of twelve, two small rooms with very few conveniences.

We came into this house the third of July I have not been into the street since, there has been a few ladies in but I have neither time nor inclination to return their calls as I do not intend to stay only long enough to make a small pile of the dust which I am in hopes at the longest will not overrun two years. Then I shall meet you forthwith. I would not have you think I am sick of my bargain not at all, we have made more money now than we could make in two years at home. I assure you it seems mighty odd to have money plenty, and when it reaches you, Ange, I want you should fix yourself and the boys up nice for winter. I want you should give the boys a present from their Mother as soon as you get the money to offset against a certain gold watch I ordered from New York which I hope will be received with pleasure. I had a present of twenty one dollars in gold for a pin, but I shall not have it made until I return, I have the promise of the best shawl that can be found in China besides thousands of other things which I should never have received had I been in the states, but after all it is the most God forsaken country in the world, not one redeeming trait excepting gold, and I want you should make yourself and the boys as comfortable as possible. If we are prospered we shall soon meet again but I think it folly to think of taking you out here, as there is nothing pleasant or comfortable here, I want you should write me every month a long letter (both of you) give me every particular but it is impossible for me to write more than one letter as I do not sit down from one weeks end to another excepting a few moments in the evening and then the room is full and I must chat or every thing is dull. I do not speak to a lady once a week. I am obliged to keep all my small talk until I return, shant I have a load. When I think of Ange and the boys seriously it seems that I must see them. I cannot stay another moment, but I fly about and drive it off as much as possible but if there is no word in the next steamer I shall be discouraged. Give my best love to Father Mother Horace and family Grandmother, Betty, Aunty, Cousins and your Dear Hus, tell him to take care of Ange and he shall have a heap. Let them have a peep into this.

Jennie

SAN FRANCISCO SEPT. 29,/49

My dear Cousin Mary & Hus.,[28]

Here we are in the City of dust not altogether gold dust but I can say to you the pan dust is as common here as shot, in the States, still money is 10 per cent per month, strange as it may seem to you it is true, & almost every thing else is in the same proportion.

There are two establishments to assay and coin gold in this place. I have seen none coined here, less than $5—business continues good, any smart business man if steady, is bound to get rich here in a short time, it make but little matter what the business is. Gambling is carried on the largest scale, from five to twenty-five thousand is not unfrequently won & lost in the turning of card, It is astonishing the amount of business done. The most busy streets in N. York will not compare with the business here; goods of all kinds, nearly fill the streets & yards, it is said by many there must be from three to five millions of money, destroyed by the loss of goods that cannot be stored the coming winter—You ask how I am doing, I can only say I have sent home or to Mr. R.D.W. Davis, No. 21, Broad street, N. York City 12-½ ounces, to [be] sent you, for distribution to the Children. Think of sending more by the next

---

28. Mary and Charles Haskell of Portland. [1993]

Steamer. (The Steamers leave this place the first of every [month?]). Please see that Ange has every advantage, encourage her to spare no pains to learn music. Please send them the love of their Father. I long to see them, hope to be ready to come home in two years. We long to be in your circle. Love to Aunt, Oliver [Reynolds] & Wife. Hope all are prospering. This moment your peaches were handed us by a friend, that were brought miles, Apples, Pairs, & Grapes are quite plenty & very good, After we have accumulated a small heap of dust, shall come home to enjoy it. Have not received a single line from the children yet. Dear Cousin write us every opportunity—it is better than gold to us. Receive this from your true Friend

T.L. Megquier

SAN FRANCISCO OCT. 31

My dearest Daughter

I have neglected writing until ten oclock and the steamer goes tomorrow but I will send all the letters to you and I think it will make one. I hope you have received the money and made good use of it, I want the boys well fixed for winter, and yourself if it takes the whole time. Johnson, now Mrs Davis wishes you to go and spend the winter with her at Mrs. Philbrooks in N.Y. after you get the boys ready for winter. You can go if you like, we will send you money if we prosper so that you need not be pinched. She wrote me she would board you for three dollars per week. Then you and have no excuse for not writing every steamer. There is nothing pleasant or comfortable now here, you would not enjoy it if here, no young ladies nothing that would delight the eye or ear.

We have got the store nearly done and it takes the fly from any thing here but it is down in town where rents are much higher than where we live, they have concluded to rent the upper story for offices, of course I shall stay in this little seven by nine a while longer. I send you a lump worth over 12, dollars. I wish you to get Betty a plain ring made as I have no lump by me now but she is not forgotten. I send you the lump worth over twenty dollars that was given me for a pin. You may get one made to suit you and have the use of it until I come, I want to see you very much indeed if I could have you for company I should be happy but it would be a great expense to get you here, and as it is rather a dangerous journey you must be a first rate girl, take good care of the boys and if we all meet again, we will journey in the states one season. I put my bonnet on last week for the first time since I have been housekeeping and walked down in town to see the store. I have so much to attend to I have no time to gad. The ladies have called on me but I do not care for society as I intend to go home when I get my pile. Give my love to Horace and family and tell him the lump I send him is but a drop in the bucket. Love to all. I send this by Mr. Calkin. He will give you all the items. I am in a mighty hurry.

From your Mother

My dear Daughter
    I have not an opportunity to write but a word. Your Mother has written. I send some specimens as you see. You will distribute them as marked. We have not had a line from you yet. If you go to N. York, be a good girl & learn. See that the boys are well clothed, give them a kiss for me. I think you had better spend winter in N.Y. &c.

From your Father

SAN FRANCISCO, NOV. 11.

Very dear friend, Milton,
    Your kind letter was received last week, there can be no estimate made of the pleasure it gave us to hear from you and others of our kind friends in W[inthrop] it being the first since we left the states. I suppose you have heard one thousand and one stories of this land of gold and wonders, they may differ widely but still all be true. Every one writes in some degree as he feels, some will get into business the moment they put foot on land, in three months will find themselves worth fifty thousand, while others whose prospects

are much brighter, will in the same short space of time be breathing their last in some miserable tent without one friend, or a single dime to pay their funeral charges, they are tumbled into a rough box with their clothes on, in which they died, this has been the fate of thousands since I have been here, yet there never was a place where money is spent so lavishly as here, it is said than one million changes hands, every day at the gambling tables. When we arrived the first of June there was but very few storehouses, all kinds of provisions were lying in every direction in the streets, carts running over bags of flour, and rice, and hard bread, pork selling at six dollars per barrel, now flour is selling at forty dollars per barrel, pork at sixty five. sugar we paid three cents a pound, when we came, is now fifty, and other things at the same rates, a pair of thick boots sold on Saturday for ninety six dollars. gold is so very plenty it makes but very little difference what they have to pay, There are but few arrivals now, some days in September, and October, there were twenty vessels arrived a day every one with more or less passengers.

The mines are yielding about the same as when first discovered but it is mighty hard work to get it, but they are bound to get it if they work, many, very many go there who never done a days work in their life, dig for a day or two without much success, get discouraged and return in disgust, say it is all a humbug, many are sick, and die there but it is not considered very unhealthy, This town is so situated when the thermometer is one hundred and fifteen in the mines there is a tremendous cold wind blowing here, I have had a fire every day for comfort, since I have been here, excepting a few days in the months of Sept. Oct which were delightful, now it is beginning to rain which makes the street nearly impassable, the mud is about a foot deep, the draymen have four dollars for a load of one hundred if they do not take it ten rods.

We have a fine store which is now nearly completed, the upper part will rent for one thousand per month a pretty little fortune of itself if rents continue as they now are, but it is doubtful, Our motto is to make hay while the sun shines, we intend to sell the first good offer and return forthwith, although there are many things here that are better than in the states yet I cannot think of staying from my chickens a long time, and it is not just the place for them at present, no schools, churches in abundance but you can do as you please about attending, it is all the same whether you go to church or play monte, that is why I like, you very well know that I am a worshipper at the shrine of liberty. The land is very rich would yield an abundance if it was cultivated, but no one can wait for vegetables to grow to realize a fortune, potatoes are twenty cents a pound, beets one dollar and seventy five cents a piece, tomatoes, dollar a pound but we have them for dinner notwithstanding, we have made more money since we have been here than we should make in Winthrop in twenty years, the Dr often makes his fifty dollars, a day in his practice then we have boarders to pay our house rent, they make great profits on their drugs, to show you some of the profits on retail, the Dr bought a half barrel of pickle in salt, after soaking them, I put up fourteen quart bottles, sold them for six dollars more than we gave for the whole, which still left me the same bulk I had at first. They are getting quite interested in politics, the locos take the lead, they pretend they are no party men, but you will find they are very sure not to have a whig nominated to fill any office.[29] The seat of government is established at San Hosea,[30] about 60. miles from this, in a most delightful spot where they have plenty of fruit and vegetables, articles which cannot be found here. I shall ever feel grateful to you and others for the interest you took in our boy, As for wages I care nothing about them, I only want him to have some employment to keep him out of mischief, if anything occurs to prevent my coming home within a year we shall send for him to come here, in the spring, but I want him treated as one of the family wherever he is. If there is no other way we will hire his board and have him go to school. We have sent some money and there is enough more where this came from. You must give an abundance of love to all

---

29. The Locofocos were originally liberal, anti-Tammany Democrats, but the Whigs soon applied the name in ridicule to all members of the Democratic party.
30. The first California constitutional legislature met at San José on December 17, 1849.

of our friends especially Sam, and Judy, if all stories are true you are getting in the same box. The Dr wants a little spot left for him. Be sure to answer this the first mail for it is the greatest pleasure we have in this country to hear from our friends. You see I am working up hill by my writing. Be sure and write and accept this from your Sincere friend

Jennie

My dear Milton, You see I am obliged to take the pen to make straight Jennie's writing. Milton, you can have no idea the relief it gave us receiving your letter. We feel under the greatest obligations to you, Br. Clark, Wing, &c &c for your and their interest in our son. We felt at rest after finding he was removed to the Dr's.[31] We wish him to have all the advantages of school that is possible, are willing to pay his board if necessary. Please see that he is well clothed good boots &c for winter, and you shall be paid in Cal. gold. We are in hopes to make our heap by spring if so shall return. Jennie wrote about provisions being high. Wages has also raised from $12. to 16. per day. Mechanics of all kinds do well, if steady, are bound to get rich in a short time. Tell Wing & Miller a ship load of good thick boots landed here now, would be worth a fortune. I think they will always fetch a good price, when the rainy season commences. Mr. Lee I think would do well here, Br. Batchelor would do well to come as supercargo with a load of boots, say soon.[32] Remember us to all our good friends in Winthrop. Tell Mr. Shaw we expect Mr. Adams in every day. From your sincere friend

T.L.M.

---

31. The U.S. Census for 1850 lists John Megquier as living with Dr. John Hartwell, the doctor in Winthrop who bought Thomas Megquier's stand or dispensary. U.S. Census, 1850, Kennebec County, Winthrop, ME, p. 24. [1993]

32. Andrew Batchelder, described as a tanner and currier, went to California via Panama in 1850 and remained sixteen years. Wing and Miller were prominent boot manufacturers in Winthrop. Stackpole, *History of Winthrop*, pp. 268, 677–79. [1993]

SAN FRANCISCO [NOV.?] 14, 1849.

Dearest Daughter

I hope you are now luxuriating upon California gold fixing up for winter, I assure you it made me feel sad to hear Johnny had not fared so well as he ought but it is nothing to what they have to undergo that come to this country, we have a young man here, who belongs to one of the first families in Boston, started from Panama last April in a little dirty schooner called the Napoleon, a very dull sailor, got out of water before they got one quarter of the way, they sent a small boat on shore to get some but the surf ran so high their boat was stove, and they were obliged to send the other to their assistance and it was served in the same way, and they were obliged to go and leave them, they put some salt port and rice in a keg with a very little water and it floated to them, it was all they had for four days a gill of rice, and half pint of water, they were all that time in a marsh of salt water up to their knees, they could not get on shore, the vines and thorns were so thick it was impossible to land, on the fourth day they found a man drying some fish, they ate and drank all night—they had to travel over 120 miles to the nearest sea port, they got on board another vessel in a short time they were put on an allowance of water, they left her the first port and travelled to Monterey, he looked so wild when he got there that he would not go in any house but stopped in the yard with the cattle, he looks strange now, this is only one of thousands.

I wrote we were going to rent the upper part of the store but they are obliged to hire so many hands it is so far to the house they board down town so they conclude to take me down there, and keep some other boarders, they say about twenty of us all, have a negro cook. I shall not have any care of the meats, your Father says I wont have to work as hard as I do now but I doubt it. I should like very much to have you here but your Father thinks it is no place for you. I suppose he is afraid you will be led astray, he has his hands full to keep me straight, if we stay another year I shall have Johny come with Mr Calkin in the spring, if we stay any more than two you and A must come. I want to see you all so much I can hardly wait. I told

Betty I had not bought anything for myself but I forgot a coarse straw for six dollars which was sold at wholesale for thirty six cents but as I had no place to store an hundred I got one and hung it up in a piece of cloth where I can look at it as I lie in bed.

I should like to have you see my cook room, in one corner I have a chest set up on end with shelves then a barrel of sugar then the door that opens into the sitting, dining, sleeping room all in one then comes a champagne box sitting on a half barrell for a rolling board then another box for the candlestick, a large shelf come next under which is a barrell of pork sack of flour a bag potatoes then the coffee mill a long board on a couple of half barrells, set my iron ware underneath the water pails and wash basin on the top, I stand there and wash my dishes, the old drake stands and looks at me and wags his tail, Mr Calkin says it is loose, then comes a half barrell of apples, then the chamber door and then an old chair with my wash tubs. that completes the first row, then sundry articles hang around such as hatchets, saucepans, gridirons slippers quarts, pints, spiders and sundry things to numerous to mention, but my chamber beggars all description. The gentleman of whom we hire the house has made you and the boys a lot of land in Boston a town he has laid out opposite Sacramento City where lots have sold for thirty thousand, they are worth one hundred apiece now so you must consider yourself a landholder. Dr. Jacob Tewksbury is here with a very pretty wife he found in Buenos Ayres had a boy born off Cape Horn and a fine fellow he is too has spent the day with me.

The weather has been very pleasant for sometime past until within two weeks it has been raining and O the mud, it is dreadful, man and beast get stuck in the slush and cannot move it is like glue takes their boots off their feet it is a foot deep, as for flowers I have seen nothing the shape of a flower but once since I have been here and those were pinks in a boquet. You must write the boys and send them this or write what of you please. Tell John we send him a lump of gold for his letter and he must write every mail. I have not time to write. I do not sit down until after eight oclock at night and three nights out of a week I have to iron. I do not go to bed until midnight and often until two oclock. Your father has sent

John some gold. His piece was so small he sent by Mr. Calkin we shall send you more soon. I want you to write Mrs. Kelly unless you see her soon and tell her all you can that will be interesting. I am in hopes to be able to write more when I get a negro to do my work. It is getting late your [Mother] sends abundance of love and you must excuse. I suppose you will go to New York. I want you to go with Betty to see Joseph A. Haines at the firm of Reed, Wade and Co. No. 15 and 16 North Market Str Boston for he has seen your Father and Mother and played a few games of whist with them. Be sure and write the boys and write every particular and when you find a place where you are contented write for your Father to get you a piano. You must learn to play.

From your absent Mother

SAN FRANCISCO, NOV 30, 49.

Dear Daughter

I might have waited until past ten, thinking the steamer might possibly come and bring me word from you, but I must give you a line every steamer whether I hear from you or no, as it is next having a line from you to write you. I think I wrote in my last that we talked of moving into the upper part of the store, which we have done and I am now safely packed away in the most comfortable place in Cal. (so all say that come to see me) though there are many that have better furniture, but we keep it warm and decently clean, a thing very rare where the gentlemen do their own work, or where it is left wholly to servants. I have a black man here, who pretends to be a cook but he dont know as much as a jackass. We had a nice thanksgiving dinner yesterday. I invited a few friends, they said they had no idea there could be so good a dinner got up, we had roast beef and veal, boiled mutton, fricasseed chicken, potatoes turnip and onions, and beet, five dollars for a poor miserable turnip, other things accordingly mince, and apple pie tarts three kinds of cake nuts and raisins champagne porter, ale, wine. I think it would make the old folks stare to have seen the empty bottles but with all their coaxing they cannot induce me to take a drop.

I have an enormous lot of room, five all told and I think if we had you and the boys I could stay this side as well as the other, there is no scandal every one is his own man, not a word about such a thing is not respectable, you know I always detested that, but do as you please, all right, I shall either send for you in the spring or come home as I cannot be from you any longer. We are having delightful weather no rain for a week, we intend keeping about 16 boarders besides our own family, they keep three in the shop, besides your Father and Richmond but I presume they all dont do as much as me, Mr Severance has been boarding with us the son of Luther Severance of Augusta but left last Saturday for the Sandwich Islands on account of his health. Uncle Horace is now here but he is going to the Islands soon, he says he has not seen a well day since he has been here, he is disgusted with the country and every thing in it. But it is a mighty busy place, it is now past midnight, I can hear guns firing, music, some calling for help. I think by the sound they are having a drunken row, but it is so common it is of no account, rolling ten pins and Uncle is snoring, it is a perfect bee hive so much noise and confusion all the time. I have starched twenty shirts this evening. I tell you this to give you an idea of the amount of work I have to do, Uncle has given me a whole piece of calico, one of de laine, one balererine. I shall make it all into broad aprons as I cannot get time to make a dress and when they get dirty throw them away as that is the order of the day in this rich country. Uncle had some washing done for which they charged six dollars a dozen, they looked so bad, he gave them two dollars to keep them.

Your Father is in bed told me to give an abundance of love and tell you to write him if you ask for a piano, you will get it sure, we intend to send you some more funds next steamer. If this reaches you in New York give my best love to all, tell Mrs. R.D.W. D[avis] that I shall answer her letter the first leasure moment, ask Mr. C[alkin] how's his back. I think you have got five cents worth. I am so sleepy, send this by one of my family that goes to Salem. You must let the boys know that you have heard from me. I will keep you writing them if I cannot hear from you I shall direct according to order until heard from,

Remember me to Horace and Father and Mother perhaps they
will open this, I would if I was them.

From your loving Mother

SAN FRANCISCO FEB 26/50

Dear Friend[33]

I know not what to say now that will be interesting after so much
has been written of Cal. but we send you a fine view of the bay, but
there is not justice done the town, you see but a very small portion
of it, and it is improving every day not excepting Sundays although
there is not quite as much labour done on the Sabbath as a few
months ago, not that (as you down east folks would say) we are
getting better but we find it necessary to have a little recreation,
such as a walk out on the beautiful hills which are now covered with
beautiful flowers and grass. (The family are constantly reminding
me that I can have an opportunity to see something *Green*) and
sometimes a game of dominoes and any quantity of small talk, as
you well know I am an adept at that. I should not think it strange
if I forget how to read as they cannot get along without me, and
they will not allow me to read in peace in their presence, and I have
given it up altogether until after I get home then won't I have a
feast after breakfast and dinner reading newspaper gossip. We are
having delightful weather for a few weeks past, business is getting
better although money is very tight. (As the business men say) and
I have been with the gentlemen so much that I can talk of nothing
but the price of lumber, rail roads, and the Town Council, the
fashions and the last conquests has no charms for me. Money is
bringing fifteen per cent per month.[34] What would you downeas-
ters think of that? lumber which brought six hundred since we have

---

33. Written on stationery lithographed in gold, illustrated on page 51 to J. Milton Benjamin.
34. For a brief discussion of the fantastic interest rates that prevailed in California during
and long after the Gold Rush, see Robert G. Cleland, *The Cattle on a Thousand Hills* (San
Marino, California, 1941), pp. 150–56.

been here is now down to sixty, a million has arrived in one day, there are a great many arrivals but most of them go immediately to the mines it is so very expensive stopping here but perhaps they go further and do worse, there is so many of my friends coming I fear I shall have some ties here to sever, a few weeks ago I could have left without a regret, but we are beginning to live like civilized beings, we have two theatres one of which we attended last week,[35] we had a box for the small sum of twenty eight dollars, it was fitted up very nice, there was a dozen ladies which is very rare to see so many at any public place of amusement.

I have forgotten when, or what, I wrote you last but I will tell you something of the floods we have had here. Sacramento has been entirely under water[36] those that had two story buildings could still transact business in the second story, those that had not, fled to the shipping, and the highlands, but an immense number of cattle and horses were drowned, they intended to levy the city at an expense of five million, quite a sum for the states but nothing for Cal. Every spot that was not overflown, they are now building cities upon, lots two or three hundred miles up the river have in [a] week gone from nothing, to thousands, every one of them at the head of steamboat navigation, steamboats are running now where in two months time they cannot get a canoe but they do not stay one moment to consider, b[u]y steamboats pay forty thousand for them, not thinking in six weeks they will have to haul up for the want of water. They are doing something in the way of cultivating the soil, by another summer, we shall have something in the way of vegetables.

---

35. The "two theatres" were presumably "Rowe's Olympic Circus" on Kearny Street between California an Sacramento, which opened as a theater on February 4, 1850, with "Othello"; and the Bella Union Hall on Washington Street. (Catherine Coffin Phillips, *Portsmouth Plaza* (1932), pp. 203–9.) The first theatrical company to play in San Francisco came to that city when it was driven out of Sacramento by a flood. The "season" began on January 16, 1850, and ended seven nights later when the treasurer lost the week's receipts playing monte! (Ibid., pp. 208–9.)
36. Floods were common in Sacramento and at times inundated large sections of the city.

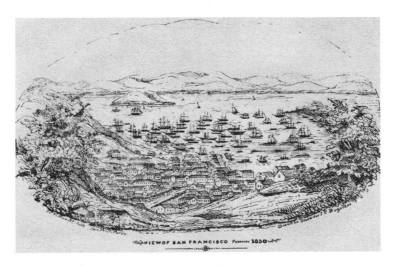

VIEW OF SAN FRANCISCO, FEBRUARY 1850.

I wish I could do justice to the political affairs of the country nothing would give me more pleasure, knowing you to be interested in those matters, but there is an old gentlemen here from the seat of government who says they are a set of lousy fellows. I should judge from what I have heard, there is not as much talent as you could put in a nut shell, the leaders are run down locos from the states the others are those who had not ambition enough to get a living doing business, and those that could, would not accept the offices, whenever they pass an act that those that hold an office do not like, they go up and make them recall it, which they do very readily, then the opposite party will give them fits, which keeps them playing see saws. The Town Council are now having very trying times,[37] they have been called upon to give an account of the funds which is a very hard matter, it is suspected they have

---

37. The first citizens' Committee of Vigilance was organized in San Francisco about a year later. For a brief discussion of San Francisco politics during this period, see Soulé, Gihon, and Nisbet, *Annals of San Francisco,* (1855), pp. 205–10.

appropriated them to their own use, as they have waxed fat, some of them say they will spill their hearts blood first. I will give you the result when I come which I hope to do before another winter. I am very greatful for your kind letter—it seems like old times to hear your remarks upon the matrimonial events. We will have a great time talking over all these things. Give an abundance of love to all, and write, as the smallest items are interesting to us what you dare not tell Mr. C[alkin], Well I leave to give the Dr. a chance.

Your sincere friend Jennie

My dear friend, & Brother,

I hardly know what to say. Jennie has written all the news I suppose, but I can say it was always pleasing to have a letter from you. [I] feel under a thousand obligations for your untiring friendship - For your attention to John, extricating him from that niggardly, half souled, scoundrel of a N__h, & other favors, money can never pay you. May God bless you & give you prosperity & health always.

I send you a specimen of gold in package with letter. It is not possible for me at this time to write more.

One thing I wish you would say to Dr. Lee Stanley. I had supposed long before this, his debt with interest would have been paid. I supposed there was property enough in Br. Burgesses hands to settle all loose debts, if properly used. I understand by Mr. Lee, the Dr. has not received one cent. I am very anxious to know something about my affairs. Will you be so kind as to call on the Esquire & ask him to send me a line immediately. Direct it in the care of C.C. Richmond & Co. Tell Dr. Lee, if not before, when I return every farthing shall be paid & I hope it will not be many months.

Give my love to Widow Stevens & Catherine & all who may inquire. In great haste from your

Friend & obt. servant
Tho L. Megquier

Dear Daughter,

We have not yet started for Maine. We heard some of our friends reported east that we probably return this month, we have not intended to state in any of our letters when we should return, could not do it if we wished to, can only say we shall return as soon as we can consistent with our interest. Our children we are anxious to see, & hope to before many months. Be of good cheer, learn a heap & see well to the boys, write them often. We have not rec'd any letters by the steamer that arrived last Sunday. We hope you will not miss one steamer.

The first of last January I sent by Capt. Wiggins $12\frac{1}{2}$ ounces of dust & some presents to you & the boys to be delivered to you in N. York if there, if not, in Portland. We are anxious to hear if it arrived safely. I wrote then to John telling him he & Arthur might go to Farmington[38] to school &c. I wrote you the same since, have them go if possible. Fearing the money by Wiggins did not arrive I shall send an order by the next mail to drawn on N. York. Your Mother will write more. Love to all from your Father

Dearest Daughter

As we received no line from you by the last steamer I have not half the courage to write that I should if I could have a long letter from you every time the mail arrives, it gives me new courage to hear from you. We now have twenty in a family. I have an Irish woman to help me, she has a very pretty little boy which makes me think of you and the boys, it hurts my feelings to hear any one speak cross to him for I think some one may do the same by mine in my

---

38. Arthur eventually did attend Little Blue, a preparatory school in Farmington. Apparently, John remained in Winthrop and prepared to be a machinist. Little, *Genealogical and Family History of Maine*, p. 625. [1993]

GREAT FIRE IN SAN FRANCISCO, MAY 4, 1850.

absence, I hope you are enjoying yourself as well as possible without your parents, I am living on the hope of seeing you all before another winter. We are having our building raised, when it was built, it was up to the skies but filling up the street has made it quite under ground, but it gives us a fine view of the bay (over all the other buildings) which is filled with shipping from all parts of the world, and makes the cook room delightful as you have a fine view. I can stand by the stove and watch the porridge and take a look at the big ships, as they are rolling lazily on the water.

We had a nice little dance the other [night] at the store of one of our boarders. I was engaged four dances ahead, isnt that smart? I suppose you will have a good laugh to see your Mother tripping the light fantastic toe. I think you must be quite lonely in the states, it seems that they will soon be depopulated there is so many arriving here. Oliver [Reynolds] has not arrived yet.

I look anxiously at the arrivals every morning for the brig Margaret, almost every week brings some of our old friends from the states. We are getting ahead of any thing on the other side in the way of improvements. We have soft water carried through the streets every day, for which you only have to pay dollar and a half, a barrel, We have three daily papers put into our door handle every morning but they are all democratic, which is quite a trouble to your Father.[39] We have concerts from Henri Herz, the pianist which are well attended at six dollars single ticket.[40] One of the boarders invited Edith and me but we were unfortunately engaged. There is also model artists but there being some suspicion that they are not all bona fide vimen it wont go down.

I want you to send this to Betty as I can not possibly write her, also write Mother, why dont she write me? I think I shant write Horace again until he writes me, as I have to write a dozen and him but one. Give love to all the relatives and friends. I should be glad to write them all but it is impossible.

Tell Charley I have got a piece of lava for him from the highest volcano in the world. The whole family will hear this and accept it as their benefit as well as yours, love to Aunty and the cousins shall write them next steamer if I receive a line from them.

Your Father is getting quite smart again but still lives upon porridge but is able to attend to business. Take good care of yourself and the boys and be sure and write every two weeks. Give us all the news.

From your Mother

---

39. "As early as 1850 there were fifty printers working at their trade in the fast-growing city. San Francisco boasted that in the mid-fifties it published more newspapers than London." Franklin Walker, *San Francisco's Literary Frontier,* (1939), p. 14.

40. The celebrated pianist gave four concerts in the National Theater in the spring of 1850. Prices ranged from four to six dollars for each concert. Phillips, *Portsmouth Plaza,* p. 212.

Dear Mother

Your letter was received last Monday by the Steamer Panama happy was I to hear from you once more, I hope it will not be so long again before I hear. The steamers are now running every two weeks and I want you to devote one hour to me that I can hear from you all, every steamer. I have an Irish woman living with me now which makes my work much easier but she leaves this week, but I do not intend to do much more work in this country, if I am obliged to stay until fall, I intend to take it easy. I suppose you will think it very strange when I tell you I have not attended church for one year not even heard a prayer but I cannot see but every thing goes on as well as when I was home. The churches are very well attended without any of my help, the baptists have the largest society in town, they give their minister $10,000 a year quite a salary but it is not as hard to pay that here, as what you have to pay yours is for you,[41] the Dr wishes me to tell you that he has been, and liked him very much. Among the many that have died in this country not one that I have heard of has expressed the least anxiety about the future which plainly shows to me that it is the circumstances that surround them that causes so much anxiety as to what will become of them after death, as it respects proffessors they lay by all outward forms of religion and have none but the vital part left, there is no such thing as slander known in the country no back biting, every ones neighbor is as good as himself, that you know is to my mind, I dislike very much to hear that this one is not respectable, or that one, when perhaps if we would look about us with the eyes of others we should find something equally wrong.

---

41. San Francisco was a city of contrasts. If her citizens frequented saloons, brothels, and gambling halls they also generously supported churches, schools and libraries.

By 1853 there were seven Methodist, six Catholic, five Presbyterian, four Baptist, three Episcopalian, three Congregational, and four other churches in San Francisco. Hubert Howe Bancroft, *History of California* (1888), VI, p. 784.

I should like to see Mr. Butler in this country, his eloquence would draw all the ladies, and his pretty wife would attract the gentlemen, in a few years he would have his coffers full, that he could lay by and rest the remainder of his days, only be obliged to attend the yearly meetings to take account of stock. I suppose that Horace will be with you when you receive this, I do wish he could have been with me when we came if he could have had his health he would have made his pile, as anything in the shape of a team coined money but the country is getting overrun with that as with every thing else but nothing would give me more pleasure than to give him a few thousands or at least to place him independent of the world. Give him lots of love and tell him if he will write me two lines I will write him six.

We are getting along about as usual have twenty in a family, money plenty, but the Dr thinks he cannot go home until he gets enough to live upon without being obliged to ride night and day but as there is many a slip between the cup and lip, we cannot feel safe at any time but they have promised me that I shall surely come home before another winter, if the children were here we should stay but as it is, I cannot. I feel as though I should fly when I think of the distance between us. Last January we sent the children $200 in dust besides quite a number of presents but we got word this steamer they were lost on the isthmus. We intended to have paid Uncle John [Cole] for Arthurs board but we made arrangements now which I think will succeed. I hope he will be in Farmington, ere this reaches you but if not, as soon as possible. Oliver is not here but the ship has been spoken on this side. He will be here soon. Uncle Horace is still with us growling about the country, fit for nothing but wolves. He intends to visit his eastern friends on his return. Mr. Benson is well and making the dimes in any quantity.

I hear Mr. Greeley has been reduced. I think the best thing he can do is to come to California.

Last night I attended a housewarming and danced all night— dont you think I improve

Whenever you have a good boiled dish think of me, not a vegetable but potatoes and those fifty cents a pound. Where is

Father? Cannot he say one word to me? I think of him often should like to make money enough to keep him in newspapers that he might have a new one every day and plenty of time to read them. Tell Arthur Mother shall give him a good hugging before another winter if we live.

Love to the Grandparents. Tell the old lady I hope to see her and take to see Uncle Hiram.[42] If she was here I would give her fifty dollars a month to sit in the chair and talk and wipe dishes. How is Jeff, and Sarah? Tell them to pick me some strawberries and I will pay them good profits I want some strawberries and cream when I come. Love to all of Uncles family and all who inquire. Write often.

Your daughter

The Dr has been out of health for two months but is better he is out now but wishes to be remembered to all.

SAN FRANCISCO, APRIL 30, /50

Dearest Daughter,

Yours of the 24 of Feby. came to us 22 April by the Steamer Panama, it was perused with great pleasure, as you may be assured they all are. It is very strange our letters do no[t] go to you more direct not one steamer has left this place without three or six letters being wrote to the states & always one to you. Last January I wrote letters to you & the boys and sent 12½ ounces of dust, a wallet to Arthur with $5 for pocket money (dollar gold pieces) & other trinkets & John a lot of notions with pock[et] money & you a nice silk dress from China, a present from Mr. C.C. Richmond by Capt. Wiggin of Bangor. We received a line from him by the last steamer, saying, our package was lost on the Isthmus, dust & all, let it go, we have more left. I felt more provoked about the presents &

---

42. Hiram Cole, brother to Mary Jane Megquier's father; lived in Lowell, MA. [1993]

trinkets than the dust. In this letter I send you a draft on Wm. H. Cary & Co. New York City, two hundred dollars ($200). Dr. J. F. Boynton (wife in Saco) left here first of last April. I gave him $100 & took his note & sent the same to Care Charles H[askell] in a letter by the Dr. to be mailed in Saco, he is to call & take up the note, as soon as convenient. Dr. B. is a fine man, he is a celebrated lecturer on Mineralogy &c., hope he will lecture in Portland. He boarded with us. I hope you have not been in the want of money. I wrote in the January letter that John & Arthur had better go to Farmington to school. Do not fail to have them go. We have written to that effect in every letter since. I have sent one thousand dollars all more of dust to New York insured, so you will not be in want for the present. Mr. Gould from Lewiston (goes home after his wife) returns immediately. Send letters on his return. I send you by Mr. Gould a silk shawl, one week from Canton & the boys each a handkerchief from the same place & a $5 gold piece for spending money while at Farmington.

Tell cousin C[harles] H. Haskell I have sent in this letter an account for him to collect, against Geo. E. Webster of Boston, brother to Mr. H. Grimes' wife. Say to Mr. Samuel G. Reed Esqr. of Boston, that Mr. Webster started from this place the 15th of January for the Sandwich Islands for the recovery of his health, expecting to return in the spring, but his health not improving much, concluded to go home around the horn, started some time in March. Mr. Grimes started for home 1st of April. No one being here to settle his business, I took the liberty to send the account to him, as I was in the want of it for my Children. If you get it & the draft on W.H. Cary & Co. N.Y. use what is needed, & please put the remainder on interest. I have written Cousin Charles by mail with a draft as yours.

Mr. Boswell sent to our house the other day for his chest, wrote a line to us sending his compliments to us, wishing us to say to his friends he [is] in hopes of getting a small pile by winter & then return home, is well, have not heard from his friends that were with him. Dr. D. Robinson arrived this morning. Not heard from Oliver since he left Valpariso, nor Lougan. Give my best wishes to Salome—her Brother James[43] arrived here yesterday, & well. Have not heard from R. Randall & Dr. Sturdefant since they left for up river. Mr. Decker, Mr. Lock, Mr. Brick & all down east [from Maine] have gone up river, as I wrote before.

We elect Mayor today, of course you will find lots of mistakes in this letter. We expect to elect a good Whig.

Give my love to all Winthrop, Portland &c.

In great haste from your Father, Ange when you put your name on the back of the draft, write it Angelina so as to agree with the draft inside. Inclose your Grandmothers letter in an envelope & send to her.

Dear daughter

I am in a tremendous hurry but I must write a line. Last night I was out to a dance until three had a fine time how we shall put in the licks on our return, the way I dance astonishes the natives.

I am writing in my little room, the ball fixins lying all about dinner half done no beds made, everything in a hubbub. The shawl is not as nice as I intended but we had an opportunity to get them for what they cost in China and they sold at auction for one hundred and seventy dollars and I wont stand any such nonsense so I took them but am bound to have a nice one some day Yours is a present from C.C. Richmond. You must write him on the reception of this.

The gentlemen are all going to make you a call on their return, they think you must be some [girl], being a daughter of mine. Give them a word for they send an abundance of love but I have not time to tell you half. I made me a white muslin with blue spots which is first rate, I expect will take the shine in the downeast diggins.

Mrs. Fred Ilsley is sitting on the trunk almost asleep but is wide awake most of the time. You must excuse me from writing. Tell Charles the males are what prevent me from writing him. Tell

---

43. James and Salome Megquier, of New Gloucester, ME, cousins to Thomas Megquier. New Gloucester town records. [1993]

Aunty Mary and Emily [Reynolds] how I love them. Write until you hear from us that we are about to start.

Mother

Dear Boys,

I have not received but one letter from you John & not any from Arthur. I wish you to write me every steamer, it not only will be gratifying to me to have the news from my native country, from your hand, but it will be of incalculable service to you. You must begin to write letters while young & in a short time it will be very easy work for you, fail not to write every steamer after this. I send this letter by Mr. Gould of Lewiston & with it I send you & Arthur each a silk handkerchief (one week from China) & a five dollar gold piece, for pocket money. I wish both of you to attend writing school when a good opportunity occurs & improve your time to the best advantage. Your Mother will write you on this sheet. I have written you by a number of the last steamers saying you and Arthur had better attend the Farmington School, for two terms, or more, say, till we return. Let your teacher find you books & whatever you may need. Be kind to Arthur & he must be so to you.

Write to your grandparents often & send my best wishes to them. Give my love to all my friends. Tell Mr. Stephen Sewall Mr. Arnold arrived here safe we expect to return in the fall.

In haste from your Father

Your Father has told you I would write but it will be short. I want very much to see you should like to have you here but you will be better where you are but if we are not there by another winter, you must be here. I cannot do without you.

Why dont you write it would give your Mother so much pleasure. If the folks all come here we will have a good time at home for there is nothing pleasant here. You must learn so you can shine when we travel. I should not like to have my boys look as though they lived in the woods and could not write their name. I cannot write now but will do better next time.

Be good boys and remember

Your Mother

.

SAN FRANCISCO MAY. 13,

Dearest Daughter

Being in haste I shall give you a short letter. Firstly Dr Robinson arrived here about two weeks since,[44] within twenty miles of this he was becalmed and went on to a small island and found an enormous quantity of wild ducks which on his arrival at this place he found would command a high price so he fixed up a boat and started the next day for the ducks, he returned with one load, but I have heard nothing of him since. The brig Margaret has not arrived yet but Capt [Frederick] Ilsley was in a day or two since says she is near here, tell Emily she must not be troubled as they are often detained by fogs and head winds for three weeks within fifty miles of here.

---

44. The Megquier letters contain many subsequent references to this gentlemen. Presumably this was the same "Dr. Robinson" who joined with the comedian, James Evrard, to open the Dramatic Museum on California Street, became the first dramatic coach in California, and satirized Lola Montez off the San Francisco stage. The *Annals* said of him, "Dr. D.G. Robinson, a proprietor of the *Dramatic Museum,* gained considerable popularity by a series of doggerel, 'random rhymes' which he gave on his own stage, in which almost every municipal man of mark was hit off, and sometimes pretty hardly too. So highly were these verses relished, and so much favor did the author gain thereby with the people, that Dr. Robinson was triumphantly returned as alderman to fill a vacancy which had occurred in the first board. He was afterwards seriously named as likely to be the most popular candidate for the mayoralty in 1852. . . . Dr. Robinson's rhymes were subsequently collected in a small printed pamphlet, which will no doubt possess much interest to such as still relish the gossip and scandal of the day" (pp. 338–39).

We have had a tremendous fire,[45] you will see an account of it in the paper, your Father has marked the situation of our place, we supposed at one time it must go in spite of fate but we have a nice iron store house on the other side of the way to which we can carry our goods for safety but you would be astonished to see the buildings that have been put up since, in a week or two more you would not mistrust there had been any trouble. I have concluded to send you Bettys letter to save writing, after perusing it with much pleasure, please send it to her. I have sent you a paper with a letter in it from Pipes, it is written by Stephen C. Massett a great musician he once composed a piece of music and dedicated it to Miss F. Williams, perhaps Cousin Mary has seen it the two ladies spoken of in the letter is Edith and me.

Your Father is quite unwell and very low spirited most of the time, if he does not improve soon I shall not wait until fall, but start if we have to leave all.

Yesterday we went aboard of the ship where Capt Mann is stopping the Capt is from Brooklyn has a right nice wife she attended the party with us her husband dont dance and mine was not able to attend but we cut around smart, perhaps you will envy your Mother but you need not, for I have to work mighty hard, and such a horrible climate, the house is filled with dust all the time a family of twenty to cook for. I have been washing in two spoonfuls of water now for two days, and many other conveniences which make it mighty pleasant. We sent you a shawl by Mr Gould which I hope will not meet the fate of your dress. The Sarah Sands has not arrived yet. I expect Mr Calkins is all out of patience, I am, waiting to see him.

Your Father tells me I must say to you that I told a fib about the flowers but I cannot get time to pick them. I have pressed a few

---

45. The fire of May 4, 1850. This, the second of the *great* San Francisco fires—the first occurred on December 24, 1849—broke out about four o'clock in the morning and destroyed four million dollars worth of business property lying between Dupont, Montgomery, Jackson, and Washington streets, and Kearny, Montgomery, Washington, and Clay streets. Many buildings were blown up with gunpowder to prevent the spread of the fire. Many of the fires of this period were of incendiary origin. See the illustration, p. 54.

but they are so delicate you cannot do much with them. You must write the boys, tell them they are ever present in your parents minds. Your Father sends much love as well as myself to all. Be sure and write every two weeks, the boarders send love.

Mother

Uncle Horace is here. I wish you would write to him.

SAN FRANCISCO JUNE 16.

Dear Daughter

It seems but a very short time between the mails on this side but an enormous while between the letters that I receive from you. I am now without help again which makes me quite homesick, the husband of the woman I have had, came back from the mines and I was obliged to give her up, We have again been obliged to pack up our duds, expecting every moment to be burnt out, but as good luck would have it the fire was subdued before it reached us, but I am heartily sick of picking up and getting ready to move, I hope my next packing will be for the states although I shall be very lonely to sit down quietly for a half day, a thing I have not done in Cal, not even an hour, you will see a better account of the fire in the paper than I can have time to give you, We were out to a party the night before the fire at the St Francis Hotel, it was quite a splendid affair your Father waited on a Mrs. Abbot and I went with Mr. Smith one of the boarders, I had me a rose colored silk, I began it one day at four oclock P.M. and finished it the next, played whist in the evening. No one mistrusted I was making a dress until I made my appearance ready for the ball.

The fire has burnt the house we had our parties at, of course we shall have to dispense with them for the present, the people are getting discouraged some of them, others are all ready to try it again, they make their money so easy that they do not feel their losses as they do in the states. Your Father bought me a watch which I intend for John, and a nice gold pen with which I am writing, I have not heard from Oliver [Reynolds] since he left for the mines, but I shall as soon as he gets located, he said he inten- (I left off to speak to someone and forgot what I was going to say) but anyway he was determined to be steady and do all he could in the way of making a fortune.

I see by the paper that Bobby is burnt out but I have not seen him Dr Robinson was going to open a theatre the next night but was burnt out, he thinks fate is against him he was going to send for his wife by this steamer but I do not know what he will do now. Edith is aboard ship with Mrs. Ilsley. I miss her very much she is very lively, always laughing, we were out in the harbor last week to a dance, had a tall time of course, I ought to write Mr. Benson but I cannot, I have so little time, but you must tell him it is impossible, I have so little time, you cannot image the tax it is to write in such a hubbub as we are in all the time.

You must write the boys and Betty and give love to all. It is time for tea. Write all the news How is mother and Horace.

Your loving Mother

JUNE 18 —

Daughter Ange,

Through the kindness of Providence we have escaped the elements but we expect our turn soon, if we should be spared, we hope to see the states this fall, if not I hardly know what we may do. I feel quite unreconciled to return without being somewhat satisfied for our trouble & dangers passed through, I assure you it looks gloomy to think of three fires so recently the whole computed at 11 or 12 million, I send one [paper] to Winthrop & Turner. You would be astonished could you peep in at one of our parties. The gaiety of dress, the lots of belles, beautiful dancers, splendid music, boquets of the richest kind, sumptuous tables, last & not least so many fine looking men. I must say in all the parties & collections I have seen in this place the gentlemen have invariably been fine looking. I fear the states have been deserted. I wrote in my last letter all of our friends from Winthrop & Monmouth arrived safe & also from New-Glo'ster & Portland, Oliver left for the mines in good spirits, appears determined to make his *pile.* I send Cos. Charles [Haskell] a paper giving a description of the horid fire that destroyed much of our city last Friday.[46] We expect a letter from you every month. When you secure the package from Mr. Gould of Lewiston give the particulars. If you are short for money let me know without fail. You can have all you want. I think of sending a small box of specimens by express in the next steamer. Give my regards to all & kiss the special friends for me.

See that the boys are well provided for. Write them often.

In much love from
Your Father

SAN FRANCISCO JUNE 30

Dear Daughter

I shall say but about three words. I am most desperately vexed that I dont hear from you, I had the pleasure of reading a line from Miss Julia Benson which told me what was passing in Winthrop. I suppose she is now in Bradford,[47] which I hear is one of the finest schools for young ladies. Perhaps you would like to attend if so go ahead, you know we want you to go where you like.

I hope the boys are well and happy at school, we have a young lad living with us from Hungary, he was one of the students that took an active part in the rebellion and was obliged to flee for his life.[48] I often think what John would have done in his situation. I

---

46. The destructive fire of June 14. It started in the chimney of a wooden bakery between Sacramento and Clay streets, in the rear of the Merchants Hotel. A high wind made it impossible to check the flames, and in a few hours the whole area between Clay, California, and Kearny streets, down to the waterfront, was ablaze. The loss was estimated at $5,000,000.

47. Julia Benson of Winthrop, daughter of Samuel Benson, a Winthrop selectman. Bradford Academy, Bradford, MA, was founded in 1803. [1993]

48. One of the many refugees of the ill-fated revolutionary movements that swept over central Europe in 1848–49. The Hungarian Republic was proclaimed in April, 1849, and collapsed in July of the same year.

fear he would not have courage, to take up arms in defense of his country at his age, he was in Vienna and left without seeing his parents, he has received a line from his parents saying whatever befel him in this country he must think himself fortunate to have escaped the trials that awaited him at home.

We are not burned up yet, but are expecting it every day, but we are in hopes to have enough left to take us home in the fall.

We are to have an eclesiastical celebration here on the fourth which seems to be a curse that follows me. We ought to have Anson, and some of the Metcalfs to make it seem like home but we are to have a ball on the third but I do not know whether I shall attend or no. I have got another woman but I do not know how she will do, but there is not much doubt but I shall have to work hard while I am in Cal,

We are improving in our streets the one we live on has become one of the busiest of the city, one morning while I was sweeping, for my own amusement I counted the persons that passed while I brushed down the stairs, they numbered two hundred and ten, the walk is crowded in the first part of the day, in the afternoon no one goes unless he is obliged too, the city is enveloped in a cloud of dust. Would not Aunty's duster be in demand if she was here? We have had lots of fun of late, one of our boarders was very much offended at another, and there was what some would call a challenge passed between them but it finally ended in pulling hair and scratching a little but it afforded us any quantity of timber for small talk.

Capt Mann is in nearly every day has got no permanent business as yet he gives me a row out on the bay any time I wish to go, it saves walking in the sand which in some places is over shoe I hope you write and send my letters to the boys as it is much of an effort for me to write.

I am now sitting on my feet, writing on your Fathers trunk as my room is not large enough for a table if it was I have none for it. I want to buy only what I cannot possibly do without, it takes all the loose change to buy white kids, ribbons, shoes, how glad I should be to receive a little package done up by yours and Marys fingers but I am in hopes to be making some arrangement for home by the time I shall receive an answer to this, but do not neglect writing until we set the time for starting home. I want to hear from Betty but I cannot possibly do more than answer the letters that I receive, excepting to you and the boys, but a mothers love forbids a steamer leaving without some token that you are ever present with your Father and Mother.

Mr. Calkin is here but has not got into business yet but is laying by for the chances, I hear that almost the whole states are coming, if so I shall be lonely on my return I want to see Horace very much. I wish he was here. it would suit him to a charm, but not one word from him or his wife but tell him I will give him a dollar a word for one long letter from him if we do not lose what we have made before we get home. Mother has not written but once. Is it not too bad? These long quiet Sabbaths, nothing to do but warm up a few beans and take care of the milk. I suppose she thinks I am very wicked but no one respects the pure religion more than myself which is to do as you would be done by. But that which says, I am more holy than thou, has no resting place in my bosom.

I should like to give you an account of my work if I could do it justice. We have a store the size of the one we had in Winthrop, in the morning the boy gets up and makes a fire by seven o'clock when I get up and make the coffee, then I make the biscuit, then I fry the potatoes then broil three pounds of steak, and as much liver, while the woman is sweeping, and setting the table, at eight the bell rings and they are eating until nine. I do not sit until they are nearly all done. I try to keep the food warm and in shape as we put it on in small quantities after breakfast I bake six loaves of bread (not very big) then four pies, or a pudding then we have lamb, for which we have paid nine dollars a quarter, beef, and pork, baked, turnips, beets, potatoes, radishes, sallad, and that everlasting soup, every day, dine at two, for tea we have hash, cold meat bread and butter sauce and some kind of cake and I have cooked every mouthful that has been eaten excepting one day and a half that we were on a steamboat excursion. I make six beds every day and do the washing and ironing you must think that I am very busy and when I dance all night I am obliged to trot all day and if I had not the constitution of six horses I should [have] been dead long ago but I am going to give up in the fall whether or no, as I am sick and tired of work, The woman washes the dishes and carpets which have to be washed every day and then the house looks like a pig pen it is so dusty, Mr. Richmond received the picture of his lady love last steamer. Give an abundance of love to all and tell Mrs. True I shall answer hers next mail if possible. Am under everlasting obligation. *Write. Write. Write.*

Ange, your Mother is so avaricious you see she gives me no chance to write except my best wishes also send them to the boys, & remember me to all, I wrote to Charles – Your Father

SAN FRANCISCO, JULY 14, /50

Dear Daughter,

Three steamers have within a few weeks arrived from Panama and no letter from you or any person from the states. We cannot think you are to blame, the disappointment is of no ordinary kind I have no doubt you are sensible of it, so much so, that you do all you can, to avoid it, Ange we still think of returning this fall. how we shall fix up our business is uncertain. 'tis good now, have escaped the fires as yet, expect every day to be turned out, if we are, it will alter our plans. It may not prevent our return this fall.

We send our box of Gold by J.W. Gregorys Express[49] & the draft in a letter directed to friend Charles [Haskell], also a draft of five hundred dollars sent to friend Charles, to be disposed of as I shall direct him in his letter. The box, after you have examined what you & your friends wish, had better be put into the Bank for safety. If

---

49. The "box of Gold" contained $1,015.99 of various kinds of gold direct from the mines, including: Feather River, North Forks, Mariposa, and Yuba. It was in lumps, dust, an ingot, and coins. "Money sent to Portland," Megquier Papers, MQ 77, 78, Huntington Library. [1993]

you get through your school at Portland, before we return, & you wish to go to any other good school, we wish you to go, & use your time in the most profitable manner—I have no doubt you see well to the boys. I think the last letter we have received from you is dated April—write every two weeks & I think we may chance to get one in few months. Give love to all.   In haste from your Father

Dear Daughter

I shall write you but little as I have nothing to respond to, and it is quite hard to keep writing every two weeks with nothing to say. We attended Dr Robinsons theatre which in my opinion was a slim affair it was merely a repetition of old yankee stories which become stale after hearing them once, and he said many things which would have offended his wife very much had she been there, but I do not lay such things to heart, but I hear he is enlarging and intends to have something worth seeing.

We had an invite to a party on board ship, we had a fine dance, and a nice supper if we do not have a dance once a week it is dull times, have nothing to talk about no fixin to do. There is to be a soiree given by the ladies of the St Francis which is said to be very select, there is quite a spirit of aristocracy prevailing here which in my opinion is composed of those that have been cramped in the states and they are the ones to set themselves up as being somebody but it is uncertain how they will succeed, at the last party they sent one home, she was taken there by an unsophisticated youth from Oregon. I think some one introduced him, to impose upon him, but he was so green he did not suspect any thing, although she kept a cigar and liquor store, but she was told the carriage was ready very soon after her arrival, I expect the ladies are trying to prevent any thing of the kind occuring again I send you our invitation to show you how we get things up here. We are trudging on as when I last wrote you promising me I shall go home in the fall but do not fail to write until you receive a line when we are to start—I want to hear from

My Dear daughter Ange,

I wrote you a long letter the first of this month, hope you will answer it by the first opportunity, your Mother wrote then & has written now & given the news of the day—Ange, if John & Arthur have an inclination to go to school, we wish that to be gratified, we will leave funds in New York to pay the bills. I have written John to that effect. We wish you to see them well fitted up if they conclude to comply with our wishes. I think the Farmington school best. It would not do so well for them to go to school together in Winthrop. We know you will give them good advice. Their books had better be furnished by their teacher. Tell the boys if you have received more presents [than] they, theirs is to come. If we prosper & return well we shall take a journey with you all, be a virtuous girl & accept this from your Father,

Give Mrs. Fillbrooks my best respects & all her family, she will no doubt take good care of you.

F.

Betty, but I wrote her last—love to her and to all our relations and friends, and tell me all the news. How is Horace's family?

From your Mother

SAN FRANCISCO AUG 14./50

Dear Daughter

I have just returned from a visit to the harbor to see Mrs. Ilsley, there was seven ladies of us had a first rate time. Yesterday we attended a splendid wedding. I presume the whole affair did not cost less than ten thousand. I will send the cards that you may have an idea how we do things here. We are getting ready for home as fast as possible, Your Father and myself think of going up the river and perhaps to the mines as I do not like to go home without seeing more of Cal. I received a line from John and Chas, which was very acceptable tell them I shall answer them probably this fall if nothing serious comes up. I dreamed Arthur was drowned which makes me shudder to think of, God forbid, that anything shall prevent our meeting again on earth.

We have not heard of Olivers whereabouts but are in hopes to when we go up river.

Mr. Ripley arrived about a week since had been very sick but was recovering he is in town for awhile. Give love to every one. Shall write next mail when we intend to start.

Your Father is well and sends love he is waiting to take this to the office.

Shall say all when I come. Your Mother & Father

SAN FRANCISCO JAN. 29. 51

Dear Daughter,

Yours of the 8th was received was very sorry you should make yourself so unhappy I think without any known cause, you must consider it is a long distance, then we were destitute of every thing to begin to keep house with and very little money. We could not collect enough to make it an object to send, I think we have been very fortunate and if no ill luck attends us we shall be with you before another winter. You send for flowers. I should as soon think of getting flowers in the desert of Sahara as in this barren country, I have not seen a flower here that is as pretty as the meanest flower you can pick up in the states, as for curiosities they are things unheard of here, excepting that of gold, and of the human species those you have in any quantity.

We had a line from Mr. Calkin saying you had not been treated well by those we considered as friends. I suppose they were afraid they would not get their pay but it is of no consequence. I ask no favors. I want you to pay for what you have and there will be no trouble. We have sent two hundred dollars by Capt Wiggin of Bangor which I suppose you will receive by the tenth of February. I think that will take you through the winter. If John concludes to go to Farmington, I should like for Arthur to go and you must see that they are well clothed by that time there will be funds that you can draw for what you need, I want you to keep an account of your expenses not that I wish you to pinch yourself but it will be of some service to us perhaps.

We have now about the same number of boarders as when I wrote you last, we have the Prefect living with us, which in Cal. is some pumpkins being the highest office in the city, a little fussy, but remarkable polite to the ladies,[50] he was formally consul, at Tahita, one of the Society Islands I have a very pretty young lady living with me from New York she came around the Horn with Richmonds uncle but was homesick with them but seems to be quite contented here with us, She ate a Philopena with a young gentleman and he got the day, and would take no present but a kiss, last night I went into my room to write, and gave him the field. I told her she might sift the flour, in the morning when the gentleman came to breakfast he looked as though he had been to mill he said she would first throw water and then flour, but he got his kiss.

---

50. Presumably Horace Hawes, who was elected prefect in August, 1849.

John Quincy [Cole] is here full of frolic. we have whist every night but I have to work hard enough t day, my wrists are getting very lame, besides I have th in my fingers, but I hope to keep up for a few mo shall give up the field to some one else. The gentlei anxious to see the daughter of your hopeful Mothe she is like her, they will take her off my hands un but it is all fun, and it does not matter what is said my love to Mrs. Philbrook. Tell her Mr. G—— neighbor and New Years day he made me a call, me with two papers of pins, I suppose that was pinning up. I want you to write Phoebe and tell h if she dont I shant bring her any lumps. I wrote Bei but I want you to let her know when you hea gentlemen who is boarding here made a bet tha lose over five thousand in the sale of lots, but h he lost ten and of course he has to bring on the ch come off to night. I have baked some molasses g some of Mrs Featherby's tarts that if they shoul I shall be prepared.

Jan. 30. The champagne supper came off noisy time we had of it, they toasted the ladi sweethearts at home, speeches, and songs, in made so much noise they disturbed the who but there was not more than three or four that they were too drunk for a sentiment, twelve to meet again on the 22. of Februa John A. Collins, one of our family, who i house near here.

Give my love to Mr. Davis and wife and te them a lump, when I come. Say to Mr. Calki he should write so few lines to send so far. I account of his reception, the effect of those he will redeem his pledge. Love to Mrs C a give me a long letter

CHAPTER TWO

SECOND JOURNEY

To San Francisco via Nicaragua
April 1852 to March 1854
Mary Jane Megquier and Thomas L. Megquier

APRIL 15TH, [1852][1]

At sea, on board the Northern Light
{In M. J. M's hand}
Very dear children

In writing you from New York I left my letter unfinished, intending to give you the particulars of our quarters on board the ship but upon our arrival there we found a perfect jam, so much so that none of our friends were allowed to come on board and I had no means of saying more than I did at the time,

My accomodations for writing are none the best, the ship rocking that I can scarcely keep my seat, with my portfolio in my lap and the noise of six hundred passengers humming in my ears, fifty two women, and forty two children, I think the confusion, when they suspended the building of the big tower must have been very

---

1. The Megquiers probably returned home in February, 1851, and stayed until Angie married Charles A. Gilson (1826–80) on March 11, 1852. Gilson owned a livery stable with his father in Portland. See advertisement in *Portland City Directory* for 1850, p. 312. In March, 1851, Thomas Megquier bought the eighteen acres of land for $600 on Bramhalls Hill, including a barn, in Winthrop where they would later build a house. In August he expanded the property for another $300. Gustavus Morrill to Thomas L. Megquier, 8 March 1851, Book 176, p. 20, and Moses B. Sears to Thomas L. Megquier, 16 August 1851, Book 177, p. 167, Kennebec County Registry of Deeds. Thanks to Arline Lovejoy for locating these and other deeds. [1993]

trifling to what we have here, some scolding, singing some relating troubles we shall have to encounter on our arrival at the isthmus, which by the way are awful, they say we shall probably be detained there a long time, as you are probably aware before this, of the loss of the North America which was to take the passengers of the boat previous, so you perceive had we gone when we wished, we should have been one of those unfortunates, so that all seems for the best so far, although there may be something still worse in store for us,[2]

Your Father and myself have a nice state room, that is, it is very cool but we have not room to turn around, it is perhaps five feet square, with my big trunk it seems impossible to get dressed but your Father gets up first and takes a promenade on deck, then by the time I am dressed it is time for breakfast and Oh! such a breakfast, my stomach heaves at the thought of it, while the little brats will eat as though they had not tasted a mouthful for a twelve month. I envy them their appetites but I can eat nothing, my dresses are getting quite loose, so soon, I think of you in your quiet little home enjoying life (I hope,) while we are panting for a breath of air, and longing for a draught of cool water, ours is from new iron tanks, which causes it to be the color of cider and unless we can get a bit of ice, it is nearly milk warm just picture to yourself, taking a glass of such a beautiful beverage to quench a burning thirst, I do not tell you this to have you think that we suffer, because we do not, but still it is very uncomfortable, having such a crowd it is impossible to have the attention that we have had formerly and I think it will be still worse on the other side as the boat is not as large as this, There are many here wishing they could have Vanderbilt in tow, by his neck for selling more tickets than he could possibly accommodate, quite a number paid a premium of fifty dollars for a state room, that have not even a berth, it seems that such things ought not to be, but I know of no remedy at present, Very many wish themselves at home they say if they had known half they would not have started. There are many ladies going out to meet their husband most of

---

2. The *North America* was lost on February 26, 1852, about forty miles south of the Mexican harbor of Acapulco.

them have children some as many as five, but not a single soul that I have ever seen before, but they are for the most part very quiet pleasant sort of people but I have formed no acquaintances they all seem to have their friends and I have seen none that I am particularly fascinated with, we therefore keep by ourselves.

As for the captain and officers I have seen but very little of them, for the first few days out it was unpleasant the last week has been pleasant and we are thinking now of reaching San Juan tomorrow night it being a new boat they do not dare put on as much steam as they will when they have tried her strength, we have run 250 miles the last 24 hours.

We are feeling quite anxious about Johny I do hope he may get a good place. The time is drawing near when Arthur will be with you. I do wish I could see you all, Bettie [Benjamin] is now among silks and laces, if not making efforts to recusitate the sewing circle and giving Bro. Sawyer a helping hand, God bless her. I would be glad to give them all a word but it is impossible at present. I thought of you Tuesday after we left but cannot bear the result at present. "We were *laying* to a *gail* of *grate severity*." Give love to Aunt, Charles [Haskell], Mary, say to Aunt there is no room for her here but will be, by and by.

You must write to Bettie and to New York, 116 Broad St. I told them you or I would let them know of our welfare. To Charles G[ilson] I would say if there is any thing the boys are in need of to look after it, and he shall be amply repaid as soon as it is in our power, I wish you to send this to Mother, I shall leave until we are in sight of land.

APRIL 16TH. 3, O'CLOCK P.M.

I have waited until this hour wishing to say to you that we are in sight of land but our boat is new, and our captain is not acquainted with the route therefore we do not get on as fast as we otherwise should, expect to get [in] sometime to night. We have had a great time to day trying to get a puff for the officers, but it was no go, and they turned it into an indignation meeting to reprove the proprietors for crowding in more passengers than can possibly be accomodated,[3] what it will amount to I cannot say, but I think about the same as all others that have been before. I would say for the benefit of Father and Mother that we have a missionary aboard who preached Sabbath day, and has a social meeting every evening at 6, o'clock which is listened to with much attention, there is beside a flaming methodist who blesses God for every comfort that he enjoys, and I presume many others but I do not chance to know them, I would like to give you an account of our fare, but my accomodations for writing are so limited I cannot do it justice. The moment the gong is struck there is a perfect jam for the dining room, if you get a chance at the table you are lucky, then you have to grab, or you do not get a morsel, I have seen four men, not one weighing less than one hundred and seventy five with their hands hold of one pudding dish pulling for a spoonful of pudding that we would not look at if at home, there is generally a row every day, they cannot get enough to satisfy their hunger but it is so little that I can eat that I do not suffer, your Father lives on rice and molasses but I have no partiality for the articles. I assure you it is very different from any thing I ever saw before. I can think of nothing but a ship load of Irish emigrants, ninety nine pigs, to one gentleman, and we have the encouragement that it will be worse on the other side but if we are well I shall get along very well, when you write to New York I wish you would tell Cousin E. I have no partiality for this route.

I would be glad to write you more but I am suffering from severe headache, thermometer at 100, the boat rocking like a cradle and not so much as a book to put in my lap, a table I have not seen on the boat, if possible I will write you from the other side, I shall expect a line from you and yours very soon after our arrival, write the boys as soon as you receive this.

---

3. Typical of the Vanderbilt policy of "the public be damned."

Betty, but I wrote her last—love to her and to all our relations and friends, and tell me all the news. How is Horace's family?

From your Mother

SAN FRANCISCO AUG 14./50

Dear Daughter

I have just returned from a visit to the harbor to see Mrs. Ilsley, there was seven ladies of us had a first rate time. Yesterday we attended a splendid wedding. I presume the whole affair did not cost less than ten thousand. I will send the cards that you may have an idea how we do things here. We are getting ready for home as fast as possible, Your Father and myself think of going up the river and perhaps to the mines as I do not like to go home without seeing more of Cal. I received a line from John and Chas, which was very acceptable tell them I shall answer them probably this fall if nothing serious comes up. I dreamed Arthur was drowned which makes me shudder to think of, God forbid, that anything shall prevent our meeting again on earth.

We have not heard of Olivers whereabouts but are in hopes to when we go up river.

Mr. Ripley arrived about a week since had been very sick but was recovering he is in town for awhile. Give love to every one. Shall write next mail when we intend to start.

Your Father is well and sends love he is waiting to take this to the office.

Shall say all when I come. Your Mother & Father

SAN FRANCISCO JAN. 29. 51

Dear Daughter,

Yours of the 8th was received was very sorry you should make yourself so unhappy I think without any known cause, you must consider it is a long distance, then we were destitute of every thing to begin to keep house with and very little money. We could not

collect enough to make it an object to send, I think we have been very fortunate and if no ill luck attends us we shall be with you before another winter. You send for flowers. I should as soon think of getting flowers in the desert of Sahara as in this barren country, I have not seen a flower here that is as pretty as the meanest flower you can pick up in the states, as for curiosities they are things unheard of here, excepting that of gold, and of the human species those you have in any quantity.

We had a line from Mr. Calkin saying you had not been treated well by those we considered as friends. I suppose they were afraid they would not get their pay but it is of no consequence. I ask no favors. I want you to pay for what you have and there will be no trouble. We have sent two hundred dollars by Capt Wiggin of Bangor which I suppose you will receive by the tenth of February. I think that will take you through the winter. If John concludes to go to Farmington, I should like for Arthur to go and you must see that they are well clothed by that time there will be funds that you can draw for what you need, I want you to keep an account of your expenses not that I wish you to pinch yourself but it will be of some service to us perhaps.

We have now about the same number of boarders as when I wrote you last, we have the Prefect living with us, which in Cal. is some pumpkins being the highest office in the city, a little fussy, but remarkable polite to the ladies,[50] he was formally consul, at Tahita, one of the Society Islands I have a very pretty young lady living with me from New York she came around the Horn with Richmonds uncle but was homesick with them but seems to be quite contented here with us, She ate a Philopena with a young gentleman and he got the day, and would take no present but a kiss, last night I went into my room to write, and gave him the field. I told her she might sift the flour, in the morning when the gentleman came to breakfast he looked as though he had been to mill he said she would first throw water and then flour, but he got his kiss.

---

50. Presumably Horace Hawes, who was elected prefect in August, 1849.

John Quincy [Cole] is here full of frolic. we have a game of whist every night but I have to work hard enough through the day, my wrists are getting very lame, besides I have the erysipelas in my fingers, but I hope to keep up for a few months when I shall give up the field to some one else. The gentlemen are very anxious to see the daughter of your hopeful Mother they said if she is like her, they will take her off my hands unsight unseen but it is all fun, and it does not matter what is said in Cal. Give my love to Mrs. Philbrook. Tell her Mr. G——- is my nearest neighbor and New Years day he made me a call, and presented me with two papers of pins, I suppose that was a hint to keep pinning up. I want you to write Phoebe and tell her to write me if she dont I shant bring her any lumps. I wrote Betty last steamer but I want you to let her know when you hear from me. A gentlemen who is boarding here made a bet that he would not lose over five thousand in the sale of lots, but he owns up that he lost ten and of course he has to bring on the champagne which come off to night. I have baked some molasses ginger bread and some of Mrs Featherby's tarts that if they should call for a lunch I shall be prepared.

Jan. 30. The champagne supper came off last night and a noisy time we had of it, they toasted the ladies the wives and sweethearts at home, speeches, and songs, in abundance, they made so much noise they disturbed the whole neighborhood, but there was not more than three or four that would own that they were too drunk for a sentiment, they adjourned at twelve to meet again on the 22. of February at the house of John A. Collins, one of our family, who is building a large house near here.

Give my love to Mr. Davis and wife and tell them I shall bring them a lump, when I come. Say to Mr. Calkin I am provoked that he should write so few lines to send so far. I expected to hear an account of his reception, the effect of those mustaches but I hope he will redeem his pledge. Love to Mrs C and the little ones and give me a long letter

Your Mother

My Dear daughter Ange,

I wrote you a long letter the first of this month, hope you will answer it by the first opportunity, your Mother wrote then & has written now & given the news of the day—Ange, if John & Arthur have an inclination to go to school, we wish that to be gratified, we will leave funds in New York to pay the bills. I have written John to that effect. We wish you to see them well fitted up if they conclude to comply with our wishes. I think the Farmington school best. It would not do so well for them to go to school together in Winthrop. We know you will give them good advice. Their books had better be furnished by their teacher. Tell the boys if you have received more presents [than] they, theirs is to come. If we prosper & return well we shall take a journey with you all, be a virtuous girl & accept this from your Father,

Give Mrs. Fillbrooks my best respects & all her family, she will no doubt take good care of you.

F.

CHAPTER TWO

SECOND JOURNEY

To San Francisco via Nicaragua
April 1852 to March 1854
Mary Jane Megquier and Thomas L. Megquier

APRIL 15TH, [1852][1]

At sea, on board the Northern Light
{In M. J. M's hand}
Very dear children
In writing you from New York I left my letter unfinished, intending to give you the particulars of our quarters on board the ship but upon our arrival there we found a perfect jam, so much so that none of our friends were allowed to come on board and I had no means of saying more than I did at the time,

My accomodations for writing are none the best, the ship rocking that I can scarcely keep my seat, with my portfolio in my lap and the noise of six hundred passengers humming in my ears, fifty two women, and forty two children, I think the confusion, when they suspended the building of the big tower must have been very

---

1. The Megquiers probably returned home in February, 1851, and stayed until Angie married Charles A. Gilson (1826–80) on March 11, 1852. Gilson owned a livery stable with his father in Portland. See advertisement in *Portland City Directory* for 1850, p. 312. In March, 1851, Thomas Megquier bought the eighteen acres of land for $600 on Bramhalls Hill, including a barn, in Winthrop where they would later build a house. In August he expanded the property for another $300. Gustavus Morrill to Thomas L. Megquier, 8 March 1851, Book 176, p. 20, and Moses B. Sears to Thomas L. Megquier, 16 August 1851, Book 177, p. 167, Kennebec County Registry of Deeds. Thanks to Arline Lovejoy for locating these and other deeds. [1993]

trifling to what we have here, some scolding, singing some relating troubles we shall have to encounter on our arrival at the isthmus, which by the way are awful, they say we shall probably be detained there a long time, as you are probably aware before this, of the loss of the North America which was to take the passengers of the boat previous, so you perceive had we gone when we wished, we should have been one of those unfortunates, so that all seems for the best so far, although there may be something still worse in store for us,[2]

Your Father and myself have a nice state room, that is, it is very cool but we have not room to turn around, it is perhaps five feet square, with my big trunk it seems impossible to get dressed but your Father gets up first and takes a promenade on deck, then by the time I am dressed it is time for breakfast and Oh! such a breakfast, my stomach heaves at the thought of it, while the little brats will eat as though they had not tasted a mouthful for a twelve month. I envy them their appetites but I can eat nothing, my dresses are getting quite loose, so soon, I think of you in your quiet little home enjoying life (I hope,) while we are panting for a breath of air, and longing for a draught of cool water, ours is from new iron tanks, which causes it to be the color of cider and unless we can get a bit of ice, it is nearly milk warm just picture to yourself, taking a glass of such a beautiful beverage to quench a burning thirst, I do not tell you this to have you think that we suffer, because we do not, but still it is very uncomfortable, having such a crowd it is impossible to have the attention that we have had formerly and I think it will be still worse on the other side as the boat is not as large as this, There are many here wishing they could have Vanderbilt in tow, by his neck for selling more tickets than he could possibly accomodate, quite a number paid a premium of fifty dollars for a state room, that have not even a berth, it seems that such things ought not to be, but I know of no remedy at present, Very many wish themselves at home they say if they had known half they would not have started. There are many ladies going out to meet their husband most of

---

2. The *North America* was lost on February 26, 1852, about forty miles south of the Mexican harbor of Acapulco.

them have children some as many as five, but not a single soul that I have ever seen before, but they are for the most part very quiet pleasant sort of people but I have formed no acquaintances they all seem to have their friends and I have seen none that I am particularly fascinated with, we therefore keep by ourselves.

As for the captain and officers I have seen but very little of them, for the first few days out it was unpleasant the last week has been pleasant and we are thinking now of reaching San Juan tomorrow night it being a new boat they do not dare put on as much steam as they will when they have tried her strength, we have run 250 miles the last 24 hours.

We are feeling quite anxious about Johny I do hope he may get a good place. The time is drawing near when Arthur will be with you. I do wish I could see you all, Bettie [Benjamin] is now among silks and laces, if not making efforts to recusitate the sewing circle and giving Bro. Sawyer a helping hand, God bless her. I would be glad to give them all a word but it is impossible at present. I thought of you Tuesday after we left but cannot bear the result at present. "We were *laying* to a *gail* of *grate severity.*" Give love to Aunt, Charles [Haskell], Mary, say to Aunt there is no room for her here but will be, by and by.

You must write to Bettie and to New York, 116 Broad St. I told them you or I would let them know of our welfare. To Charles G[ilson] I would say if there is any thing the boys are in need of to look after it, and he shall be amply repaid as soon as it is in our power, I wish you to send this to Mother, I shall leave until we are in sight of land.

APRIL 16TH. 3, O'CLOCK P.M.

I have waited until this hour wishing to say to you that we are in sight of land but our boat is new, and our captain is not acquainted with the route therefore we do not get on as fast as we otherwise should, expect to get [in] sometime to night. We have had a great time to day trying to get a puff for the officers, but it

was no go, and they turned it into an indignation meeting to reprove the proprietors for crowding in more passengers than can possibly be accomodated,[3] what it will amount to I cannot say, but I think about the same as all others that have been before. I would say for the benefit of Father and Mother that we have a missionary aboard who preached Sabbath day, and has a social meeting every evening at 6, o'clock which is listened to with much attention, there is beside a flaming methodist who blesses God for every comfort that he enjoys, and I presume many others but I do not chance to know them, I would like to give you an account of our fare, but my accomodations for writing are so limited I cannot do it justice. The moment the gong is struck there is a perfect jam for the dining room, if you get a chance at the table you are lucky, then you have to grab, or you do not get a morsel, I have seen four men, not one weighing less than one hundred and seventy five with their hands hold of one pudding dish pulling for a spoonful of pudding that we would not look at if at home, there is generally a row every day, they cannot get enough to satisfy their hunger but it is so little that I can eat that I do not suffer, your Father lives on rice and molasses but I have no partiality for the articles. I assure you it is very different from any thing I ever saw before. I can think of nothing but a ship load of Irish emigrants, ninety nine pigs, to one gentleman, and we have the encouragement that it will be worse on the other side but if we are well I shall get along very well, when you write to New York I wish you would tell Cousin E. I have no partiality for this route.

I would be glad to write you more but I am suffering from severe headache, thermometer at 100, the boat rocking like a cradle and not so much as a book to put in my lap, a table I have not seen on the boat, if possible I will write you from the other side, I shall expect a line from you and yours very soon after our arrival, write the boys as soon as you receive this.

---

3. Typical of the Vanderbilt policy of "the public be damned."

Give much love to all our friends. That you both may be happy
is sincere wish of your Father and Mother

{In M. J. M.'s hand}
Dear Children
   When I wrote you last we were expecting every moment to see
land, but did not until Saturday morning when the Captain was
going to shove us ashore without ceremony but the passengers
rebelled said they should not go, until the small steamer came from
up river to take them off. but the Captain gave them nothing to
eat, and Sunday they all went on shore, but your Father and myself
found a friend in the captain of the coal ship that came alongside
and he invited us to stop with him which we were very happy to
do, as the accomodations were very limited on shore, and such a
crowd that is was difficult to get any shelter for your head, To give
you an example of the meanness of our captain. Captain Lee whom
you have heard me speak of seeing in San Francisco had just thrown
his lines on shore to tow his vessel in to unload coal for the steamer
when we went into the harbor, our Captain called him to come
alongside which he did where he waited until Sunday night for
them to unload when the Capt of the steamer told him he did not
want any coal, very soon there came a squall, and they cut us clear
and we were in great danger of being driven ashore, if we had gone
the vessel would have been lost, and the steam company would have
her to pay for, I assure you I was not a little frightened when I heard
Capt Lee threatening to shoot if they cut the lines, the wind
blowing a gale I thought it might be our lot to know what it was
to be wrecked on a foreign shore, but they soon got their anchor
out and we were all right.
   Monday morning Capt Lee kindly put us on board the Edmund
Miller to take us up the river and we avoided the crowd on shore
which was awful indeed, many waded in the water up to their
middle, and paid five dollars to have their luggage put on board,

they feared very much to be left in Graytown, it was said to be unhealthy,[4] But about noon we got clear and started up the river San Juan which is not much different from the Chagres excepting it is much larger, it is considered perfectly beautiful but the heat and musquitoes are such a trouble that I could enjoy nothing, The first night your Father and myself sat on the fly fighting musquitoes and panting for a breath of air, women and children so thick we could not stretch our limbs, neither of us had a wink of sleep, we got as far as we could go, in that boat quite early in the morning but the passengers would not start until their baggage could go, therefore the last of them did not get off until Wednesday morn, we were put on a large launch to take us over the Mazuka rapids where it took eight men to row us one mile and a quarter, and were three hours in doing it, we then went on board the Sir Henry Boliver which took us to the Castilla rapids where we had to walk a short distance around the falls and then took the steamer Director where we again had the pleasure of sitting on the luggage without any sleep. I was so bitten by musquitoes you would not recognize me if I could have made you a call without your expecting me.

Thursday morning we went up river about 12 miles where we met the Central America were one night on her lying on the open deck nothing under us but your Fathers coat under our heads, and crowded to death and burning up with the heat, and you cannot get a mouthful of food excepting what you take with you. I assure you I got heartily sick of hard bread and sardines. Thursday night we crossed Lake Nicaragua and went on shore at Virgin bay. Friday morn took dinner at the American Hotel and your Father took a survey of the town and found us a nice little place kept by an New England man and as pretty a little wife as you ever saw, we had nice ham and eggs and chicken hard bread and milk in our coffee a luxury we have not known since we left New York, every one that called

---

4. Greytown was a British protectorate. Cholera and yellow fever were the most dangerous epidemics. The town was nearly wiped out in 1854 by an American captain in retaliation for an insult to the American Minister.

on us was delighted with our chance and they urged them to take the wife, and daughter of that flaming methodist I told you of in my last, but the trials and fatigue of crossing has taken the jingle all out of him, he is a quiet as an infant asleep, And yesterday morning which was Monday we mounted our mules for crossing had a nice ride over none of the troubles of bad roads notwithstanding many of the ladies fell off, one hurt her eye badly but I know of no serious accident and we are now on an old brig halled in shore for the accomodations of travellers, there are eight of us ladies down in the hold lying on boards covered with the dirtiest blankets the rain pouring down, there was not a dry thread in my blankets this morning, We have to pay four dollars per day, have nothing that is fit to eat but eggs, and so much crowded that [there] is not a chance for you to sit down excepting the little spot you occupy at night, In the morning I pile up my carpet bag, blanket and shawl and sit down for the day, Your Father takes his meals on shore, found an old acquaintance who gives him a cot in his office but he keeps so many game chickens that he gets no sleep after two in the morning. I assure you we are in a great muss but hope to leave soon.

Dear Children
It is a great task to write in this now wet & hot country. Your Mother has given you the particulars as far as possible, pen cannot describe our journey as it [is]. We thought it hard before, it is doubled & more have had rain showers of rain, the one today is very oppressive. It is a matter of uncertainty when we leave this place, we hope you will not neglect to write by every mail, we are quite anxious to hear from you. Arthur will be with you soon. John I hope has obtained a good place, hope to hear how you and Charles get along. be economical as possible, be industrious. I hope Charles will find a good place in the church & attend meeting constant on the Sabbath, be good Children. Give love to all.

in haste from your Father

The steamer Pacific has arrived this morning and we are in hopes to be off to day but I anticipate a regular quarrel for many have tickets for state rooms on deck, and there are none there, but as good luck will have it we have one in the cabin, There is not an hour in the day that I am not thankful you are not here, many things I would like to say to you all but time and paper will not admit, as our trunks are at the store house, I can [get] no paper or clean clothes, we are as dirty as any old washwoman but I am looking forward for better times, Say to the boys they are ever present with us. Give abundance of love to all. Tell Mary I shall expect a line from her, Write to Father and Mother of our whereabouts. I am aware that you will have a tax to read this but I write sitting on a blanket and the rain wetting my paper. Much love to Charles Angie Johny and Arthur.

Mother

SAN FRANCISCO MAY 15./52.

{In M. J. M.'s hand}
My dear Children

We are as you see in this land of wind and dust once more, I suppose there has been great changes but we have not been long enough here to know them; as for myself I think the city does not look as well as when we left but that same eternal wind is blowing yet. I have written you the particulars of our journey to the Pacific, if you do not receive it, I can give it to you again for it is written upon my memory at the enormous expense of twenty pounds of my corporosity, which give me the trouble of taking back the surplus I gave my dresses before I left.

We arrived here the 13th after a most uncomfortable passage owing to the crowd of passengers and taking fifty from them, the remainder ought to be put upon some desolate island 50,000, miles from any civilized people, for they cared for no one but themselves and not enough of that to keep cleaner than our yankee pigs; it was with great difficulty you could get sufficient food to satisfy the cravings of hunger, they would appropriate the contents of every dish, to themselves before a decent person could get set down to the table, I think a famine must be the result of an immigration of so many gormandisers upon our unfortunate city;

Where do you think we heard of the favorable result of your city elections? Off the island of S. Margaurita about 1,000 miles below here,[5] your Father chanced to hear some one speaking of a paper they saw in Acapulco which was left by the Tenesee two days before, giving the news from the states up to the 9th of April, I would gladly have sent up three cheers for you on the broad Pacific, But no; I would not have the good city of Portland applauded by such a race of boors, I think echo would not have responded to the hurra's of such a lubberly set of donkeys therefore we talked of the pleasure you and Charles H[askell] and Mary, would have, and perhaps indulge in an ice cream or an oyster stew, and should not we like to have taken part with you; broiling under a hot sun, impossible to get either food or drink enough for comfort?

We are now at Mr. Calkins very comfortably situated Mr and Mrs Davis, Dr and Mrs. Robinson, are boarding here, they are done with theatricals for the present, he is going into the auction business with Mr Calkin; Uncle Horace [Cole] is in the city now, he is engaged in quartz mining extensively, enjoys good health. Sam Barrett was in this morning looks finely says he was never better situated than now, I told him he must go home and see his Father and Mother. He told me he would try to, in the fall, he is a clerk on the Antelope running to Sacramento, John Q[uincy Cole] is well Lougan Mr. Weeks Mrs. Moody, all well, Mrs. Davis tells me that McLellan does not treat his wife well, but I cannot vouch for the truth of it.

Mrs Richmond has gone home and I presume will say that Cyrus is all he should be, but she has not had one moments peace since

---

5. The Island of Santa Margarita, off the coast of Lower California. Later the scene of the wreck of the *Independence.*

she left the states, she has been in tears most of the time and it was with the greatest difficulty that she could get any thing to wear and he never took her out at all although she may say to the reverse, as for himself he is a perfect sot, as proof of it, I asked him what steamer his wife went in, he told me the Golden Gate. I told him I thought it was the Northerner, and he could not tell which, he told me [he] bought a state room for her, but a gentleman that boards here says he did not that he gave her barely money enough to take her across with the strictest economy,

Your Father has done nothing towards settling, as we have not been here long enough to get rest from our journey, but by next mail I hope to give you the particulars and send something for you and the boys. I do feel very anxious for you all especially Johny, how disappointed if I do not hear by mail. I want to say a word to all but it is impossible we have so many calls, and the mail closes tonight and your Father is waiting. I have heard nothing from Oliver but hope to before another mail.

The ladies all send abundance of love to Charles and Angie, and the boys, Mrs. R[obinson] would give a word if there was time. Do give love to all, and remember that Mother must hear likewise Bettie

Your Father & Mother

My Dear Angie[6]

I do feel very much oblige to you for the reading of this letter from your dear Mother. I have been exceeding anxious about them and hope I shall now be as truely thankful to the great God for preserving their lives through so many dangers. Oh that God may still bless them.

We are all well we are anticipating a visit from you & the rest of the friends from P[ortland] soon as the strawberries are ripe if they are as plenty as the prospect now is they will be abundant. I shall write to M E soon and let you know when they will be

---

6. This letter was written on the back of the May 15, 1852, letter by Mary Jane Megquier's mother, Rebecca Cole, of Turner. [1993]

ripe. You must be ready at a minutes warning. We shall have some dressmaking for you to do hope you will be prepared in mind as well as boddy to do it.

in haste your Granmother

SAN FRANCISCO MAY 30TH/52

Our loved ones at home,

Yours of the 20th, was received and it will be useless to say how much pleasure it gave us to hear of your happiness and comforts. We feel quite anxious about John but when we hear that he is in a way to get his grade and we are able to remit you money to make you all comfortable I shall feel much better about you. We have been here now two weeks, your Father has been using every means in his power to get a settlement with Richmond,[7] but until two days since he could not get a sight of him, he would get a horse and drive out of town and stay until after dark, at one time he was gone three days and no one knew of his whereabouts, when he came home he was dirty, and ragged, had filled his pockets with eggs which you know is not a very safe place, and he does not know where he has been and can give no account of himself, therefore your Father was obliged to sue for a settlement, the sheriff was two days in search of him whose fees with the lawyers amounted to one hundred and fifty dollars, so much for lawyers in Cal, but now they have left it to three disinterested men and are under bonds of 10,000 to abide by their decision. I assure you we are right glad to get out of the clutches of the law, there would be no more left of us than the Kilkenny cats when we got through.

We are still boarding at Mr Calkins and enjoy it as well as I could any where to be doing nothing. The old stand is unoccupied but I think it wholly owing to Richmonds mismanagement, he was so unsteady no one would trade with him and such a consummate rascal no one would rent a building of him could they possibly avoid

---

7. Cyrus C. Richmond, Megquier's partner. [1993]

it, no one can do business with him to the amount of five dollars without having a quarrel with him, but he said it was because business had left that part of the city, therefore he took a store in another street, but he has not paid his expenses since he returned, he is now sick at the old stand and those who tend upon him are obliged to give him stimulants to prevent the delirium tremens, it is sad to look upon him, such a perfect wreck, but I think we shall do something smart as soon as we can get matters straight,

Dr Robinson and his wife are boarding here, they have been unfortunate, she at one time had a salary of $150 per week for playing at the theatre but it was so much against her feelings they gave it up, but the Dr is in for any thing but fortune has not considered him one of her favorites as yet, she is now sick with the chills and fever, she takes great interest in your welfare wants to see your Charles exceedingly, I think she is not very happy here although she says but little, but it is surely a hard place unless fortune sees fit to smile upon you.

I have seen many of our old friends since our return, all seem to give us a cordial welcome, they advise us to make Cal. a permanent residence, but never shall I give up the idea of making that nice little farm my home at some future time, but if we have our health it will not be until we can carry out our plans in some measure.

This morning Mr Calkin and myself took a walk onto the hills, we strayed into a Chinese Hotel where were hundreds of Chinese with their luggage which consisted mostly of baskets with covers, the entrance was like a church open with a gallerry closed up, with windows to look into the main entrance, The proprieter took us into his private room, and showed us a flag he had received from home, it was twenty feet long and twelve broad of the nicest crape, crimson, the design of an immense dragon, wrought with gold thread, the same on both sides, like the shawls, with enormous eyes gazing at the moon, and some chinese figures, making the most magnificent thing of the kind, I ever saw but there is no place in the world but this where there is wind enough to float such an extensive affair. I thought of you, what an addition to your cabinet. I hope to be able to send you that box at some future time.

Yesterday Mrs Davis, Mrs C. and myself took a walk out to happy valley where we saw some beautiful flowers, pansies, gillyflowers foxglove of every color and hue, grass pinks by the cart load but one solitary rose, but it was a beauty, it reminded me so much of home I could have shed tears but it is of no use to indulge in those things in this country. Mr Merrill with whom we boarded when we first came to this country is cultivating a garden, he wished me to ask you to send him some heliotrope and some geranium seeds a very few in a letter. I priced one small pot of pansies, it was six dollars. I think you and Mrs Hopkins could make money if you were here selling sponge cake and boquets.

I wish you to say to Mrs Smith that we used every effort to find her husband but was not successful, I took the liberty to open the package thinking there might be a letter but as there was none, I left the papers on the table and someone appropriated them to their own use and yesterday the brother called and said her husband had gone to the mines, was well when he heard from him. I told him that he must send word, that his wife wished him to come home, I met the lady she introduced to me who went to New York with me in the street but she was looking another way and I was in haste therefore I did not speak, her Uncle has a beautiful house and I presume she is very happy. I think our friends in Maine are well as I have heard nothing to the contrary. I have heard nothing from Oliver [Reynolds] have made inquiries from all I have seen in Marysville. I hope he is at home well and happy. Mrs. Davis says she feels quite flattered to have a namesake but thinks it will be a long time before she will be able to visit you in Maine. Give love to Mrs True, say that I have inquired for her benefit the price of lessons in music which I found to be three dollars a lesson, We hear Mr. Beede is well and doing well. Give my love to Mrs. Ilsley tell her Edith is still enjoying single blessedness has her house furnished nicely. Capt Long and wife board with her they have a fine boy Mrs. Tewksbury would have had one but it was in too much of a hurry to get to Cal, she is comfortable the other ladies of her acquaintance are well. Mrs. Smiley is trying again to see who she can do, I shall look for the Grecian soon.

I think our little Arthur is with you now and Bettie will be with you when you receive this and poor John where is he, how I want to see you all, I hope when next I write to give you a better account of our business. Mr. Weeks is going to pay us in a short time and we shall send something a soon as possible. Your Father is writing to Winthrop sends much love. I shall write Mother remember us to all as I cannot mention them. I leave it for you to do. Charles I would say it gives us much pleasure that you do not regret the step he has taken and it is my most ardent wish that your joys may ever outweigh your sorrows, when you see C. Megquier, ask how Mr Dow succeeds, for me.

Do not neglect to write. Tell Mary [Reynolds] that [the] apron is not forgotten. I shall expect twenty when we get housekeeping tell her there is a fat English Capt here that wants a wife and he has got the dimes. John you must write your Father and Mother and you Artie Charlie, Bettie and Angie

Your Mother

Your Father wishes you to tell Clark Megquier that Morse has sent the money and gives directions to have the note taken up.

Capt. Mann arrived to day with a cargo of Chile women, A lady told me if I would put the flowers I wished to press between a number of folds of tissue paper, then press them with a warm flat iron until every particle of moisture was dried away they would retain their color. I know you will say I hope Mother will experiment but I cannot promise

SAN FRANCISCO JUNE 30TH/52

Dear Children

Another two weeks has passed and we are still waiting for some turn in the tide of affairs, Mr Richmonds death has placed his business entirely in the hands of one whose honesty never will kill him, he has his money and wont pay out until he is obliged to which is any time within a year, which places us in no enviable situation, though we are by no means discouraged, but I want very much to be able to send you a draft occasionally that you and the boys may be indulged in some things which perhaps you do not in reality need. I am aware you are well provided for, but still I know you would like a little purse of your own that you may be independent. I suppose you will get a little money from New York before this reaches you to remunerate you for the boys fixins. I am very glad John has an opportunity to pay his way, if he was here he could get a hundred dollars per month, and if we have to stay a long time, I must have you all here, for there is no pleasure in being so far from you. Every steamer that leaves brings home so vividly to my mind that it appears to me I must go, I cannot sit and look upon them any longer if I had any thing to take my time that I had no leisure to think, I should feel better. Your Father has purchased a bedstead and mattress, so much towards housekeeping and a box of port wine for me to treat my friends with I wish you would step in and take a glass.

You say H. Bachelder[8] and Mrs Smith are on the way. I hope Henry will have a good time, of all troubles in this life keep me and mine, from having any care of a woman and children coming to Cal, I heard a number say that a cool thousand would be no inducement for them to undertake it again.

The boat we came on has come again, she reports the S.S. Lewis at San Juan del Sud, she came in the day before they sailed, she will probably be here in a week as she has to stop at Acapulco and clean her boilers after so long a passage, her passengers were very uneasy and threatened to take the Pacific, not the ocean, but the Steam Ship of that name. I suppose Mr Clark is on her, Mr Bodge was in yesterday, says Mr Beede is well and doing very well, they are running the same coaches that Mr B used to run through Winthrop, their line is from Stockton to Moquolumne Hill a route of about fifty miles.[9] He gave a strong invite to make them a call thinks they

---

8. Henry Batchelder, son of Andrew, was twenty-two in 1852. He stayed in California until his death in 1888. Stackpole, *History of Winthrop*, p. 269. [1993]

9. The Bodge and Beede stage line supplied one of the seven daily stages that ran into the city of Stockton. Seventeen public houses served the travelers on the fifty-mile-long Mokelumne Hill Road. The road crossed the Calaveras River at the Davis and Atherton Ferry, a few miles east of the town of Bellota.

will go home in two years. We have an addition of two spinsters to our family in the capacity of country school marms, one is particularly nice, when she came down to the table this morning she said she did not see how they could dispel the illusion that it was going to rain, all looked as though there was to be a shower of smiles but as good luck would have it some one brought up a new subject and all went well. Mrs. Robinson is housekeeping but I think domestic cares will not sit as lightly upon her as some I could mention. Your Father and myself called upon them, it happened to be their dinner, they all jumped but the Dr. like a parcel of frightened children, one of the gentlemen gave up his dinner entirely.

We are now having most unpleasant days the wind is blowing a gale to day such a dust you cannot open your eyes. I wish I could have a run in Debbies field and pick some strawberries. I wish you to write Mother as I innocently mentioned a box of wine in this, and do not want to add one other pang to the dear old lady, and still another thing that would be awful to her, your Father has got to be a smoker. He is now lying on the bed smoking a cigar, waiting for this line.

I have just had a call, it is so late I must leave you. Do give the three boys much love. Why dont Mary write me, give love to her and all the family, you do not say whether Oliver is home or not. Not one word of Emily remember me to her and Bettie is not forgotten.

Adieu all the loved ones

Jennie

I can assure you it is very gratifying to us to hear from you & home by every steamer, as we have thus far, we hope to hear more particularly from the farm after you have visited it, not a word yet about poor Dick & the two pretty cats, to say nothing of the colt & cow. I have written Mr. Morrill, Mr. Wood, Milton [Benjamin] & others & hope to have a full detail of events in a few weeks. The particulars could be very amusing to us, as it is somewhat uncertain when we can return, our business moves very slow, The settling of

R's [Richmond's] estate is done by law & in this country it is for the lawyers interest to prolong it as much as possible that their fees may be enormous. The making and serving a writ cost me over $155. so much for beginning a settlement with Richmond. it was lucky I did so. it brought him to an arbitration, which it was thousands in our pocket, when we get it. We are here just in season. a few weeks later, nearly all would have been gone. he was completely thunderstruck at our arrival. he had done & was doing all he could to cheat & gouge even to forging accounts, &c, &c, we are now waiting for Mr. Plume, his executor, to pay us our dues & unfortunately he has the power to keep us out of it nearly a year & I think him mean enough to do it.

I sent some money from N. York to Charles. I hope $255—but $55 anyhow—use it for the boys. I have sent Charles a Chinese pamphlet, please send it to Arthur. Give our best regards to Father & Mother & Sister Gilson & all, tell Charles to kiss Mary for me—
In haste from your Father

SAN FRANCISCO JULY 12TH/52

Dear Charles, and Angie

And still another two weeks has passed and we are no nearer getting into business or getting home than when I last wrote, our hands are completely tied. Mr. Plume will not sell the house, or rent it, and says he shall do nothing for six months, so you see there is no probability of our seeing you at present, I assure you it is no very enviable situation to be placed in, but if we have to stay longer than spring I shall have you here and give up the states for the next five years, your Father shakes his head, but it must be so, I cannot endure the thought of the boys being homesick and no remedy for it, we had a line from Johnny saying he never was so homesick in his life. I felt as though I must go to him but on a second consideration I thought I never would go until we were abundantly able to carry out our plans at home.

Mr Clark arrived last week, he intends to sue the company for not coming up to what they promised, I think it high time that something was done to prevent so much imposition upon the public.

Mr Lee and H[enry] Batchelder came last Saturday. Mrs Smith did not come, they complain of hard fare on the other route, they are however looking very well

I received a line from Mother by Mr. Clark, she says she does not expect to hear from me in any way except she gets a line from Mr. Clark. I do not know why the old lady is doubtful of my attentions as I always answer all I get from her, because I have no love for the good town of Turner she thinks I care for none of its inhabitants, and if Father, Mother and Horaces family were out of it, I should never trouble myself to visit it, and I should want a tremendous smart horse if ever I was compelled to drive through town, that I should have no opportunity to call up old reminiscences.

Dr Robinson is still at his old tricks humbuging the world, After he left the theatre he went into the auction business where he undertook to act the country greenhorn, but that did not take with the business people and he was obliged to give it up in a very short time, Now he is preparing patent medicine, comes out with flaming advertisements, where an angel is coming from above and presenting a bottle to a poor miner bent nearly to the ground by disease, and says he has orders from Oregon to Cape Horn and it is only two weeks since he began, it knocks pepsin in the shade. Mr Stewart has made us a call. He is now at Bodega[10] about fifty miles from here, in a tannery, says he is doing well his hair curls as nice as ever.

Mr and Mrs McLellan called, she is looking very well and he was dressed in the tip of fashion but still you could see the country gawk sticking out. Lugan is there in the kitchen, he has lost six hundred dollars by Robinson, money that he worked hard for.

---

10. Site of a Russian settlement and trading post in Sonoma County. Bodega Rancho was granted to Stephen Smith, owner of the first steam grist and saw mill in California, in 1844.

Dr. Tewksbury and wife are well, she is as pretty as ever, he is in company with a Doct. Rowell from Gardiner, Me, he is a fine looking young man, quite a ladys man, A married lady cut a lock of hair from her head and took particular pains to curl it up and put a warm flat upon it making it look mighty nice and sent him, and he was hard hearted enough to send it back, Was it not awful; but that is the way they do in this country.

I think I wrote you in my last that we had a maiden lady boarding here, last Saturday eve I think she had a bite; but whether she will succeed in pulling him in, remains to be told but we are all looking forward with considerable anxiety. it would be such a nice thing to have a wedding here for we are sometimes hard up for amusement, the weather is so unpleasant we do not go out but little, and the gentlemen are tired after dinner so they sit down and snooze until dark then some of us take a game of whist while others look on or go down street or to bed, so ends the day.

Edith is not married yet Mr. Sutton takes quite an interest in her affairs, goes to market, looks out for a servant carries home the bundles, what will come of it I cannot say. Give my love to Mrs. Ilsley tell [her] I am inquiring every day if the Grecian has arrived but the ships all have a very long passage this season, tell her Mr Watrous is very much obliged for what she has done for him shall be there forthwith.

The gentlemen here have concluded 2,000 is fortune enough to make a splurge upon in the states, as the people are very ready to magnify it into 100,000 and upon that they can marry an heiress, and some unlooked for event has prevented them from receiving their dues from this country, and of course their wife will hand over, and they can lay back and take comfort for the remainder of their lives, so you perceive you are bound to be victimized. We are going to write John not knowing how to direct, we send to you, therefore I will leave fearing there will be nothing left for him. Give love to Aunts family. We hear nothing from Oliver. We have written to Mother.

Yours Affectionately
Jennie

{In T.L.M.'s hand}

Dear Children,

We must acknowledge you have been very kind, in writing every mail & I can assure you it gives us much pleasure to hear from you every two weeks. Your Mother says if we stay longer than next spring, you all must come here. I think she is somewhat visionary about that. The dangers of coming would not pay. If Charles is doing well, making a fair profit, it will do better than coming here, business is so divided now, it is not of much account. I wrote in my last E.H. Merrill would send you $55 or $255 soon- if either way, let me know.

Your Mother is now living high, green corn, string beans, tomatoes, green peas, apples & pears in market-but unfortunately the wind blows severely, even now— Do not fail to write us every mail till we start for home. We have received Arthurs letter by Mr. Oatman, called on Mr. O. at the Rassette House-not in, have not seen him yet.

Please give my love to all & accept the best wishes from your Father & Mother Megquier

{In M.J.M.'s hand}

Mr. Oatman called last night, was very well and wished to be remembered to you, said he promised to write Charles but he must excuse him this time he had so much to write otherwheres, says he likes very much if his goods were here now he could sell them to good advantage. Last night we heard of the death of Mr. Lord of Bangor, son-in-law of Gen. Vezie He had but just arrived here the second time. He was moving some luggage on board the Gov Dana which contained a pistol, It went off and passed through his side, he lived about 24 hours, it will be a sad thing for his wife, he had quite a family of children.

Remember us to Father G's family

{In T.L.M.'s hand}

I send a newspaper please do the same by us. Mr. Barrett is well, says he [is] going home to marry a Maine girl.

{In M.J.M.'s hand}
My very dear Children

We received yours of the 20th of June, to day at noon, and I was in a tremendous hurry making a travelling dress to wear to Sacramento. Mr Barrett was up this week and invited me to take a trip with him, and unfortunately we were just making preparations to go to housekeeping, After making a tremendous splurge about selling the property they have found they cannot sell without the consent of the heirs, and your Father has concluded to rent the building for awhile therefore I shall stay but one night then I must take hold of work again. I assure you I am quite tired of play, We have purchased some cane seats sixty dollars per dozen rocking chair twelve stove fifty, other things in proportion when I get settled I shall give you all the particulars

Tell Mary I shall answer hers next mail, her letter was a jewel in our estimation. Poor Mrs. Spear came for the sole purpose to die with her husband.

Perhaps I will be home in time to write you more but I am in such a haste I can think of nothing. I will leave for your Father to finish. Do give love to all write the boys.

{In T.L.M.'s hand}
Your Mother you perceive has started a letter & left it for me to finish. You also see by her own writing she has this day left my bed & board & gone up country with a young man, & I must say with as fine & good looking young man as California can produce, hence I am perfectly satisfied, you must inform his Mother. We are now making arrangements to move on the old place on Jackson Street next week, as there is no probability of finishing our business very soon. law must have its course. It was very unfortunate for us he could not have lived to settle his business, or left it in different shape—he had laid every possible plan to cheat us out of every cent, but they were not deep enough, although I think he would have

succeeded had we not come out—In this country, a person must attend to his own business, or it is not done, I am doing some business in my profession, take as much cash in one day as I could in Winthrop in one month. we intend taking a few choice boarders, which will we hope give us a good living while we stay—

Mr. Oatman called on us the other day & wished us to send his love, saying he would write next mail, he is looking very well, likes much, has made a short journey up river, will probably settle there.

Tell Mrs. Ilsley Jennie is watching every arrival hoping to see her husband. I expect they intend having a great time, tell her not to be alarmed, I will see to them. Tell Aunt, if she was only here, she could make her fortune. a nice old farmer in Nappa Valley has applied to us to look him up a neat tidy wife, about her age, What shall we tell him? Our friends are very anxious we settle in this country & send for our children, If we do, we shall expect all of our relatives, Hattie & Mrs. Becler &c &c. Mr. Becler is in fine spirits & doing well, have not seen him yet, hope to, before long. Mr. Clark is in this city yet, watching the chances, in good health & spirits. I noticed the other day when reading a letter from home his eye was quite moist.

Heavy guns are being fired all day on account of Scotts nomination. We shall do all we can for him, although, Daniel [Webster?] is our choice—In an hour or some over, a large lantern sign was painted & erected over the Whig printing office in a conspicuous place on Montgomery street, excitement great, one man had his arm blown off & much injured other ways.

Dr. Tewksbury & wife are well & doing very well. I see Miltons Brother occasionally, is well & as industrious as his father— Your Uncle Horace sends love, says you must write him a long letter after visiting the country & getting well satiated with strawberrys & cream. Our market now is overrun with pears, melons of all descriptions, weighing from 40 to 75 lbs. & over—tomatoes not quite as large as your head, beets over two feet long, weighing over 75 lbs. squash, unaccountable—Apples from Chile. Capt. Mann brought us in a load the other day gave us a fine lot. Strawberrys & Blackberrys gone long ago—I intended to have filled this page but having a violent headache, shall be obliged to close, all send heaps of love. Remember us to all especially to Father & Mother Gilson & Sis, a kiss from me. Write often to the Boys-& I remain your affectionate father

TLM & Mother Jennie

SAN FRANCISCO AUG. 13./52

Our dear Children,

We have with much pleasure received a letter from you on every mail to this time. The mail steamer that has been due for some days has not arrived, 12 o'clock noon. We are expecting a letter by her. Cannot answer that until next mail. We are now fairly underway keeping house full of boarders except two - have Uncle [Horace] Cole, Mr. Oatman, Mr. Chapin, Mr. Snell, Mr. Daniels, Mr. Hodge & Mr. Merwick If you and Charles were here to take our spare room, we should be full, if you come soon we will keep it, please telegraph or send Charles & Mary [Haskell], & say to Aunt [Mary Reynolds] she must come soon or I fear she will lose her chance to become a California Million-heir.

The death of Henry Clay struck a gloom over the whole country. his funeral obsequies were observed in the City on Tuesday last the 11th,[11] It was admirable got up, all put on deep mourning, almost every nation helped form the procession, between two & three miles long, all the public places, horses & carriages in the procession, were dressed in the most neat, becoming & elegant mourning possible, The Oration by judge Hoffman, on the Plaza, *it was good,* tears flowed freely, The procession formed at 9 o'clock morning, commenced their march, passed through some of the principal streets

---

11. Clay died June 29, 1852. The funeral oration in San Francisco was delivered by Judge Ogden Hoffman of the United States District Court. The oration survives in printed form. Judge Hoffman's *Report of Land Cases . . .* is a standard work on California land titles.

& to the plaza. The oration was short, it terminated at 3 o'clock, P.M. They were from 9 A.M. to 2 P.M. marching to the Plaza—
We intend to elect Scott & Graham. The Locos pretend to [be] pleased with their nomination though they feel greatly chagrined at his, Pierce, fainting one day on the field of battle. They say here he sprained his knee, or foot[12]—I hope Maine will do her duty & go for the Whig ticket entire I send you a paper, please send me one in return. Mrs. Dean spent part of the day with us, sends love. Samuel Stanley arrived here from Marysville a few days since looking well, says he will stop here, if he can find something to do. Mr. Weeks & wife & daughter are at Mr. McLellan's, well, except Mrs. Ws little girl has Dysentery, is very sick—
Being at this time pressed with professional duties must close. Your mother writes.

Give love to all. In great haste
From your Father T.L.M.

{In M.J.M.'s hand}
Your Father has been these two days giving you the news of the city and I supposed there would be nothing for me to say, but in looking it over, I find he has given you none of the particulars of housekeeping. It is now two weeks since we came into the house it being on the same spot of the old one and a facsimile in form. I feel quite at home but it was a sad looking place, being unocupied and left very dirty but in three days I got it cleaned and was ready for boarders, I wish you was here to help me with my sewing I am obliged to take mighty long stitches.

---

12. The Democratic nominees were Franklin Pierce and William R. D. King. Pierce, a brigadier general in the Mexican War, had been prevented by accident or illness from taking part in any major engagements. The Whig candidates were General Winfield Scott—"Old fuss and Feathers"— and William A Graham. Pierce and King won the electoral vote of all but four states.

I have it for one evenings work to make a sheet and one pair of pillow cases. I do not get my dishes washed after dinner until eight oclock, we breakfast at eight, lunch between twelve and two, dine at five and often have five changes of plates which you are well aware gives quite little pile of dishes.

We have collected a little money that we did not have to run in debt to begin, but it takes a mint to begin, we have to pay $28. per dozen for the common wooden chair and $60. for cane seats, every thing in proportion. It grieves us much that another mail leaves without taking any funds for those poor boys but we cannot get one cent from the executor to send, but I am working very hard and by the next steamer we hope to send some to clothe the boys. If you do not get any from New York, I know not what you will do, your Father says if he cannot collect by next mail he shall hire some as John Morrell must have some anyway. I get up every morning by five and go to market where I meet all the negroes and spanish in town. I do not like it but your Father cannot tell what is wanted therefore I must do it. When I am writing you I think I cannot stay from you any longer. I must go home, but while I am in the kitchen, I am so very busy that time passes rapidly. Tell Mary that I cannot say when I can answer her letter, these few lines will keep me in the kitchen long after it is dark. Give love to all our friends. Mother must not be forgotten. Poor Johnny, my heart aches for him, my feet trouble me, I have been doing nothing so long, now I do not sit down excepting to my meals.

Dear Arthur I must give him one word. Say to Charles we have taken Mr. Oatman under our wing. He wishes to be remembered to him.

The ladies are all well here and are very happy to hear that you think of them.

I wish Bettie was here to dust and help me laugh occasionally. Uncle is with us and would like much to see you says if you are like your Mother you are a plaguy smart woman, would write you if he was in better plight says he is in hopes to get money enough to buy powder to blow out his brains, I want you to write John and accept the fondest wishes of your Father and Mother

{In M.J.M.'s hand}
Our loved ones at home

While the family are taking their lunch I will give you one half page which must suffice while I have so much housework to attend to, It is as rare as hens teeth for me to get one moment to sit down, We have now a Chinese boy to scour the knives, if he should be contented we shall take him home, Your Father thinks he is not good looking enough but if he is a good servant it is much better than good looks, he cannot speak one work of English therefore he cannot tell how old, he is about the size of Artie.

We have a gentleman and his wife boarding with us which brings the family to ten, and how much I wish that it could have a certain five I could mention added to it, but now I feel as though I must see you, If Charles could be here now with a small investment in quinine, and cologogne, he would make his fortune it is now bringing sixteen dollars an ounce, but by the time he could get it here others would do the same and it would be sent home again as it has been done before

Your Father sends a little money. I want you to be paid for what you expended for the boys and get them what they need for winter. If you cannot make their shirts, get Mother to do it, and pay her well for it. Mr. Barrett has just been in and says there is a prospect of his coming home this fall. I think he has his eye on P. Long if she gets him she will get a prize.

I have no time to tell you more. If you want to hear more, you must ask questions and I will answer them short hand. Love you know to all

{In T.L.M.'s hand}
I have inclosed in this a draft of $300 on the Atlantic Bank, Boston, from Page Bacon & Co. You will please take up a Note of $100. John Morrill (our tenant) holds against me & pay him $50. on acct., & pay the remainder of Rev. Mr. Sawyers bill which is 10

or 15 Dollars, & Mr. Thurston's bill which is, I think, $8. The remainder you will keep, for the boys. You have no doubt by this time received $55. from E. H. Merrill, N.Y. money I paid here for the son of Mr. Potter of Brooklyn, & it is barely possible $200. more may be sent from E.H.M., if so, use it. The $3375. due from C.C. R[ichmond]'s estate, I cannot get at present so you perceive it impossible to set the time start for home. Your Mother's little Chinese boy is very industrious. We received a letter from John the last mail dated July 15, but none from you. I can assure you it is very odd not to receive one every mail, don't fail.

What do you suppose Artie writes John: "To be a good boy & stick to his business so as to get a good trade, be steady & go to church every Sabbath," *very good.* We were much pleased to see your letter dated Winthrop, though not word about the aqueduct, whether sun, or the pear trees in Hawses garden, or when the piany in said garden was carried to the farm & living &c. We anticipate the next letter will give it in full. Susan Sears arrived here safe & looking finely, about 10 days since—Mr. Oatman is fine fellow, is well & writes by this mail. Charles, please keep a regular account of what you do for the boys & we'll make it all right when we return—

Give a good hearty kiss to your Mother, sister & Angie for me & I will return yours to Jennie & regards to Father. Write the boys often.

Mr. Beede is well, doing well & in good spirits & Mr. Budge also, was here last week.

Love to all of our good friends & cousins & a kiss for Mary [Haskell] & Aunt & be assured we remain you affct. Parents

M.J. & T.L. Megquier

SAN FRANCISCO, NOV. 30,/52-

Our Affect. Son, Charles,

Your of Oct. 17 arrived here, Nov. 20th with Betties, Johns & Arthurs, for which we were pleased & very grateful, on the sixteenth of Oct. last I sent you another check of $200. on the same bank as before, & loaned Mr. Potter of Philadelphia $55. who agreed to send to E.H. Merrill & he to you. It probably will come, sooner or later. I wrote Mr. P. & sent the order Nov 1st. You wrote me you had been to the farm & settled with John Morrill satisfactorily.

The reason I did not leave the business of the farm with you in the first place was, I thought it would be too much trouble it being some distance & take too much attention from your own business & hence I spoke to Milton [Benjamin] & told him I should write him the particulars, & did so, but did not receive any answer for a long time, then I wrote you & in connection with Milton, because he was on or near the spot & could keep an eye on the premises.

After writing my wishes about the farm, I think I finally left it for you to do what you might think best, & I think on the whole your plan the best, with this alteration; let Deacon Cole take the cow, if he will, or some other one, & hire the colt wintered & pay the money & let the hay in the barn remain & if it is thought best in the Spring to sell, do so & not have it taken out by small parcels & by different persons. If you have not found a tenant before this, you had better write Milton, (If it is not already done) to have the barn fastened up securely & windows boarded. The large outside cellar door should be fastened on the inside, by going down through one of the scuttle doors in the stable—it should be fastened very secure, because it is quite liable to be blown down by a heavy wind, besides the snow is liable to press it in. The blinds on the barn, especially on the cupala should be hooked to & secured. I wrote Milton on the first of Sept. to look after the farming tools & other things that were liable to be wasted, together with my carpenters tools, when John left the premises. The most I feared from shutting up the barn was from unruly cattle getting in & destroying the nursery, & apple trees, knowing John had done no fencing, & also knowing part of the fence on the road was miserable & far from being safe. I wrote John Morrill to be sure to leave the fences secure, but I think he must have left before receiving the letter. The board fence from the field bars to face wall on the road, I put up myself, only temporary & if it has not been made over or secured since, it will not be safe through the winter. Mr. Sears cattle are very unruly, as it may be too late to repair fences before receiving this, I can think of no better way than for Milton to hire Thomas Sears to see that no cattle intrude on the premises. As you did not mention Miltons name in your letter, I suppose you did not see him when there, if so, he had not received my letter because I wrote you & M[ilton] on the same subject. I wrote him to secure the refusal of what manure would be needed on the farm (to be hauled on in March) which could be ascertained from Morrill. I wrote him I would send him funds, will you please see that he has funds for that purpose & remind him of my wishes if he has not received my letter. My whole object in hiring John last season, was to have the line & road fences made perfectly secure, & I shall not think the nursery safe till done. I think you cannot do better than to pay Thomas Sears something to see that the bars & gates are shut & fences secure till spring & then I will have them made secure, if we do not return which is impossible now to tell, our affairs move along very slow. Plume still holds on to the money due me from the estate & likely to, till April. Rain is falling every few days. It is now very muddy. The hills & vales are looking quite green, flowers will soon begin to show themselves, fine grapes still in the market.

You say Mrs. Richmond talks coming here. She is a very foolish woman to so do, she cannot gain one dime by it, & her expenses will be great, & she cannot board with us.

You say of yourself & Angie that you are enjoying first rate health, & that Angie never looked better. Charles, we had & still have, perfect confidence that you would take the best care of our daughter, & we hope she will return it, with double interest. Tell Angie to continue in good spirits. It is only a Mothers fate.

Thank Bettie a thousand times for her kindness & tell her she shall always be remembered by us. Let her not work too hard. Love to all. Your Mother will write a line—adieu from you friend & wisher T.L. Megquier

It is but a line that I have time to write my boy has been sick since Thanksgiving but it was not overloading his stomach. I thought much of you on that day. What a change since the last. Would not Miss Angie have drawn down the corners of her mouth had we foretold her what would come upon her. I should much rather been at Readfield to a nice ball than where I was, true I had a span of roosters and some ducks plum pudding, squash pie cranberry pie but all did not make up the absence of our children. Mr. Oatman was here and Capt Mann who sends his regards to all. Johny, I wish you were here but we cannot decide upon anything at present and dear little Arthur. I look upon our boy and think what would he do in China among strangers who could not understand him not a friend to look to, sick as death.

Mrs. Robinson is having her parlor finished and thinks she shall receive calls New Years day she speaks of you whenever I see her likewise Mrs. Davis and Mrs. Calkin. What in the name of common sense does Mrs. Richmond think we care for her coming. I can assure her we cannot get our dues much more anything that belongs to her. I am very glad to hear that you were pleased with your present and I do wish you had sent me a ribbon by mail as I am very much in need of one and I think yours very pretty. There is a very nice white thibet hood and coat I wanted to get you. I suppose it would take a cool hundred but it is splendid. What is your opinion about it? Oh! Bettie, Bettie, how I want to see you all.

SAN FRANCISCO DEC. 15TH/[1852]

Dear Angie,

When this reaches you I hope you will be freed from your trouble in part, altho it will increase your care I hope it will give you much joy.[13] I do wish to be with you more and more every day. We

---

13. Angie and Charles Gilson's daughter, Jennie (1852–1943), was born on December 24. [1993]

received yours in due time saying the boys were both with you. I hope John will try and do something to pay his board and dear little Arthur must take care of the baby for his. My little China has recovered much to my joy. I was almost of a mind to beg out sometimes there was so many things to be done. There is not a thing of interest to tell you. we are having a sewer laid on Jackson St., which makes it delightful, mud four inches deep on an average all over the house which I assure you presents quite an *aspect.*

Kate Hays is still singing here draws good houses every night.[14] I have not heard her as yet but it is not that I am not invited. There is a young lady boarding at Mr Calkins who came out about three months since and is now preparing to marry an old bachelor and as ugly looking as time besides, but he has got the dimes, she is nineteen. he has made her a present of a set of diamonds, Davis not wishing to be outdone has made his wife a present of a pin two hundred and fifty, it is in the form of a loop with ends with an opal in the center. She is having a white damask to be married in, but when she comes to set down and look him in the face she will be sick of her bargain. Mr Johnson is having some little bundles of laces and ribbons coming every mail. I wish you would occasionally send me one. I do not wish you to find the funds only send me something and take the pay from the deposit.

It is very cold now and have been obliged to have a stove in the sitting room which your Father did not like to do as he expect to be turned out when the building is sold, which will be as soon as the power of Attorney arrives, which we hear Old Mrs Richmond has consented to give, after hearing that it would not benefit us particularly. I am sorry that you have the boys just now. I hope you will remunerate yourself from the available funds and when those are gone we hope to send more but it is hard times here now but little business on account of the rain provisions enormously high, your Father is decidedly blue.

---

14. Kate Hayes, referred to as the "Swan" or "Nightingale of Erin," probably the most popular of the concert singers of the time both in San Francisco and the mines.

There was an execution here last week, the gallows was first erected in plain sight from the house, but the people objected to it, and it was removed, the first one in the city, excepting those by the vigilance committee and rumor said he would not have been hung had he not been poor.[15] You perceive I have obtained some small sheets to avoid sending any blank paper but is it time for the mail to close. The friends tell me to give you an account of the floods and fires, but I cannot, so farewell

Your Mother

Mr. Oatman is now here and is quite well, wishes to be remembered to you. Regards to Mother and intended to have written but cannot this time.

SAN FRANCISCO DEC 31 /52

Dear Angie

I am now sitting at the little round table with Mr. Becler on the other side writing to his dear Lucie. It is desolate and gloomy enough, raining all the time the whole country flooded which renders it impassable for man or beast, and the miners are nearly starving, owing to the speculators buying all the provisions made them so enormously high that the up country people thinking it might come down; neglected to lay in their winter provisions, and now it is utterly impossible to get it at all, and they are getting desperate taking provisions wherever they can find them; whole trains have been drowned. One man lost six thousand head of cattle. Mr Beede and Bodge are in the city now being obliged

---

15. The story, including the removal of the gallows, is told in the *Annals of San Francisco*, pp. 409–10, in some detail. José Forni, a Spaniard, was executed for the murder of José Rodríguez, whom he claimed he killed in self-defense. The gallows was first erected on the summit of Russian Hill and then moved about a hundred yards to the west. A crowd of from six to ten thousand persons, men, women, and children, witnessed the execution. See the illustration, p. 111.

to haul off their teams on account of the mud.[16] for two long, long weeks we have scarcely seen the sun. I am obliged to dry my table cloths by the fire which makes a pretty mess of it, Tomorrow is New Years, the gentlemen make calls on that day and the ladies keep a table loaded with cake and wine. I suppose three quarters of the gentlemen in town will get most essentially tight. I shall not make any special preparation but I have baked some cake if any body comes. I do not want to be piggish.

Tuesday eve Mr Snell took me to the concert to hear Miss Hayes, we had a nice time although she cannot compare with Jenny, nor has she the compass to her voice that Madame Biscacianti[17] has, but it is very sweet and she is much better looking.

I likewise had an invitation from a China man to attend a chinese theatre but it rained so incessantly that it did not play, and I will send you the note I received from him, he is said to be a wealthy merchant, but I know nothing of him, he has the charge of our boy, O that I could look in upon you. I imagine you lying on the bed in the corner Grandma sitting before the stove trotting the wind out of the baby Bettie down stairs looking after the tea things as it is now three oclock here, it is past six with you. Now for the farm. I want you to look after it, as though it was your own. If your Father hires a man I want you to make him do as you wish, I want you to get all the shrubbery you can set out upon it. I for one do not intend to go home until we get something to live upon, for here I can have what money I wish to spend altho' I have to work mighty hard for it, but it is nothing to being pinched, and I want the farm improving and if we do not come at all it will be yours, now do not feel sad at the last remark, but when I hear of so many dying from home, I think perhaps it may be my lot, but I hope for better things. I called on Mrs. Robinson. She is working very hard for her but the Dr says doesnt. We are supporting ourselves, Mrs R. put my old

---

16. Heavy rains frequently shut off all communication with the diggings and stopped mining operations. At such times the mining communities suffered acutely. Beede and Bodge, as mentioned in a previous letter, ran a line of stages from Stockton to Mokelumne Hill.
17. Elise Biscaccianti. A rival of Kate Hayes for popularity both in the cities and the mines.

trimming in my hat. I told her I would not buy a new one as I was expecting Angie to send me one and if you have not sent one, you can put it into a cigar case. I wish your Charlie to purchase [it] for me and send by the next mail after receiving this, none of your muggins kind, but a right nice one as I wish to present it to one of my friends. I wish you to avail yourself of the funds in the treasury to satisfy, if there is any, if not there shall be some soon.

Give love to Mary and tell her I felt mighty cute, that I had written her before I received her last, and shall answer that soon. I think it a great treat. I see you received a diploma for the moss cottage. I suppose you will have it in a gilt frame and hang in the fore room looking as though you had been made a member of the foreign missionary society. In the distance, speaking of the cottage reminds me strongly of two cats who used to circumnavigate its interior much to the discomfiture of its fair owner. Now Johny, Arthur, Charlie, Bettie I do want to see you all but I am glad that you are not in this gloomy place at present and that you may all be happy is the earnest wish of your Mother

Love to all.

SAN FRANCISCO JANY., 15, 1853

Father Cole,

I intended to have written you a long letter before this, but circumstances, together with a disinclination one in this country has of writing, is the apology.

In a few days, after our arrival & was somewhat rested from our journey, I commenced arranging my affairs with Richmond. I soon found he did not intend doing anything towards a settlement without being drove, would go off and stay two or three days at a time & when I did see him, he would make some flimsy excuse for not meeting me according to agreement.

I finally set the day & hour, after which I should not wait any time, but should carry him through a course of law, till he should be satisfied. The time passed, no Richmond. I went directly to a lawyer, got a writ, put it in the sheriffs hands, watched for him nearly three days before he was to be found.

After finding himself sued, he cowed down & wished to have the business settled by arbitration, each choose a man & they the third, if necessary.

I told him it was the course I had been trying to take ever since I had arrived & would do so now, if he would come under a bond of $10,000 to abide by their decision, & that the suit would not be stayed till he did. He signed the bond, our arbitration went on & he died Wednesday after the bond was signed Saturday. They made my account against the estate $3,375 & a lot of land on Jackson Street & real estate being on the rise, I shall not offer it for sale till spring, if then we can sell satisfactorily, we shall pick up our duds & start for home. We still remain at the old stand have a few boarders, do something in my profession & on the whole take more money in one month here than I could in the states in two years, This is decidedly a great country, the soil here is exceedingly rich especially in the vallies, wheat, barley, potatoes, onions, turnips, cabbages, beets, radish, finally all vegitables grow in abundance, a wheat crop is not called good, unless they get 100 bushels to the acre, & potatoes a peck in a hill pumpkins four feet long, that I have seen, squash weighing 75 lbs. water melons 40 to 60 lbs, beets four feet long, weighing 40 lbs, an English turnip that could not set in a ½ bushel, that I have seen—handsomer & better flavoured pears I never saw, than are grown here, no good apples yet, but in the Northern part of the state I think they are bound to have the best of fruit in a few years, We have grapes in great abundance, They are in the market yet, I saw a lot to day, which is on the fifth month since they first began to be brought in to market, provisions of most kinds are high now, flour $40, beef 3/per lb, pork 4/6 per lb., mutton 6/per lb. chickens 12/a piece & poor at that, turkeys at Thanksgiving time were $10. a piece—

Late in the fall, wild game is very plenty, a few miles from the city, the creeks & low lands about the bay are literally lined with them, they are shot by the dozens, & brought to this market, so are ducks, plovers, snipes, quales, cranes, white pokes, & I think I have seen in the market every kind of birds that ever flew, or swam, it is all right, if it is only a rare dish, you say then, California is a great agricultural country, I say the land is uncommonly rich, but I think it must be always subject to drought, fires, & floods, the latter at this moment covers nearly all the vallies; thousands of heads of cattle have been drowned within a few weeks, one man came to this City the other day that lost 11000. head, stock next season must be high, I hear a man from Maine has gone home for the purpose of buying 3000 head of cattle & drive them across the plains, if he should get them here safe his fortune is made, You have no idea the distress in this country now, a fire in Sacramento City,[18] then a flood, has bankrupted many, & has deprived the farmers of putting in their wheat crops early, which may prove an entire failure, so you perceive this country depends entirely upon circumstances, if favourable all right, if not, the reverse—Up to this time the rains have outdone/49—which was considered at that time uncommon, Sacramento City was overflowed, the old Californians said. Such a freshet had not occured for seven years before. They say (the Californians) it is all owing to the Americans, & they say (the Mexicans) soon they expect to see the Americans come to this city on whales backs. This was directly after they saw one of our steamers come into this bay—I must say it is surprising to see the emigration at this time, four steamers have arrived within ten days with 400 passengers each. These, together with those that arrived here around the horn, is enormous, & most of them without money. I am told hundreds are exposed to the inclemency of the weather every night. the halls of every hotel are full every night, & many have no chance to lay down, even on the floor, we are looking for a heap of suffering before winter closes.

It is impossible to set any time when we shall return, not till we can finish our business complete, Mr. Richmond made his will

---

18. Sacramento, like San Francisco, suffered frequently from destructive fires, some of which were clearly of incendiary origin. In the fire to which Megquier probably referred, hoodlums were starting fresh conflagrations in various parts of the city with burning shavings while honest citizens were fighting the main blaze.

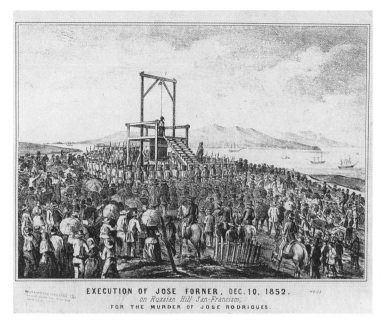

EXECUTION OF JOSE FORNER, DEC.10, 1852.
on Russian Hill San-Francisco,
FOR THE MURDER OF JOSE RODRIGUES.

EXECUTION OF JOSÉ FORNI, DECEMBER 10, 1852.

before leaving New York, which gives his Executor one year, to settle the business, which deprives me from the use of the money, which is worth from 3 to 5 per cent per month.

We hear from Horace occasionally by way of Dr. Parker, we have not heard directly from Horaces wife & children but suppose they are well cared for. Jennie often speaks of them, give them our best regards with Sarah Jef. Philo call[ed] on us a short time since, is well & in good spirits, speaks of home with a moist eye. Our [regards] to his wife, Uncle John & Aunt Sally [Cole] & the girls – Deacon give my special regard to Deacon Merrill & wife, hope she is enjoying better health—Jennie & Myself send much love to you & Mother Cole, adieu. In haste from your son Thos. L. Megquier

The writ & other expenses were $200. We heard of Hirams death by way of Portland & were not much surprised. We hope his family will do better without than with him, remember us to them. Oliver Reynolds we have not heard from except by the way of Portland we fear he has lost all wish for home.

SAN FRANCISCO JAN 30TH/53

Dear Angie

Two weeks have again passed and we are still enjoying pleasant weather, business improving but my chance is ever the same cooking and sweeping, employ most of my time, occasionally I get half an hour to sew, I have to sit on the bed to work, as my room is not large enough to admit a chair, as I have not any thing new to write you, I will try and give you a concise description of it, I think its length is ten feet, breadth six, We have a nice large maple bedstead with a spring bed, a husk mattress, a straw bolster, and moss pillows, which are very nice, then your fathers trunk stands at the foot and we are obliged to push it under the bed a little to open the door, mine stands next the partition which gives us scarcely room to squeeze through, my dresses with your fathers clothes are hung against the side of the partition at back side of the bed, my bonnet is tied up in red silk hankerchief and hangs on a nail quite as contented as if it was in a band box, under the bed we have a demijohn of brandy a skull of a flathead indian, the bones of the head of some fish a carpet bag filled with trash, a candle box filled with pieces of dresses, a case of jellies, Ahook's bed which consists of numerous blankets and comforters which he removes every night to the dining room, and lying on your fathers trunk are blankets and pillow with which I make a bed on the sofa for a gentleman who stops here about half the time, and I am sitting on my box of patches with my paper on the bed, your father lying down with his feet over the foot board puffing like a steam engine, and I was right glad when he fell asleep for he was full of questions and I was obliged to tell him I should leave before he could stop his talk,

I have got my shawl rapt around the ink bottle to prevent its tipping over. Now is it not an india rubber room to contain so much? There is a rat who make us a visit every night and helps himself to whatever he can find, he tears the paper from the wall for a nest, your father constructed a trap of a half barrel but he does not see fit to climb up the barrel for the sake of being drowned.

Kate Hayes is still singing here draws very good houses, there is quite a feeling existing between her friends and those of B————, Robinson is still composing and singing songs, Last Saturday eve they called him out a second time. he told them they need not make such a fuss, it was nothing to what he was going to do Monday night, he was going to have two or three farewell benefits (it was a take off to the lady singers) he had been improving his voice by putting it in soak, his wife and boy are well, always inquire for you.

I do feel very anxious to hear and likewise to see you but I do not want to go home without a competence, here I can have as much money as I wish to spend and almost any time can send you a hundred dollars if necessary but I am very economical. Your Father has given Potter sixty five dollars to pay his passage home around the horn and if you should be fortunate enough to receive it you can buy some frames for the portraits unless there is some more important call for it.

Tell Johny the watch is hanging in our bedroom but we think it will not be best to give twenty five dollars to have it taken home, but it will go the first opportunity. I hope he has got something to do as it is not pleasant to hear that he is doing nothing. I suppose he can only write when he has one from us but he must consider how many we have to write and so little time.

Poor Longley he must suffer in his feelings. I should think he would come here which would seem to be a solace for all such trouble as his, Mr. Oatman is quite well is flourishing around town today in a new pair of plaid pants which he says he believes set rather snug. We had a line from little Arthur he says that he had a fine vacation but his account of the cats at the farm was anything but pleasant—poor things, is it not too bad they should starve, how I wish I could have them here, do you know there are but few people in the state of Maine I would give more to see than them. I shall say nothing of my expectations in your next—fearing all will not be well and it will pain you. Give much love to all our friends, Shall write Bettie if I have time.

Your Mother

Monday night I had intended to write Bettie and Mary but I have been trying to wash but had so much company that I have done nothing. Tell M. I found the cousins on the hill well and pleasantly situated on a sand bank. Mary Annah[19] left here today for Sac[ramento]. She is well.

SAN FRANCISCO FEB 15.TH/53

Dear Angie

We congratulate you in the happy termination of your troubles and I do not doubt you enjoy all you say but still it is an enormous tax to take care of them babies but I do sincerely hope she may be spared to you that we may have the pleasure of seeing her there is not an hour passes but I think of her and all of you. I have been quite sick with the dysentery but have done all the work but there was times when I would have given a great deal to have cuddled into my own bed on the farm and have you and Bettie ask me what I would have, of course I should say nothing; but I did dread my work prodigiously. I am better but not well. I am very glad when it is bed time. I wanted to send baby a present but I know of no chance to send and I have no time to go out and look up something but it shall go soon if I can get out to find any thing.

Edith Sherwood is at last married her husband went to the states the last steamer and they were married the evening before, not a soul knew a word of it until after he was gone they think they worked the card beautifully. Uncle Horace is still with us looking for the chances. John Q. says he has three things in view either will

---

19. Mary Annah Cole, sister of John Quincy Cole. Stackpole, *History of Winthrop*, p. 334. [1993]

bring him a mint, if they do not drop which in all probability they will. I have often heard him speak of a certain ship load of goods that were consigned to him that would have brought him a fortune but they must take fire and burn on the Missippi about a year since but the last mail brought news that all was not right and the parties were liable to have a steady home assigned them for some time but he cannot believe that Lyman is guilty, he feels quite sad about it.

Dr. Robinson talks of going to Australia, he was going to give them a song a few nights since when the stage manager came forward and said that he was not able to sing on account of it, they infered from what was said that he was over the bay, if so Mrs R will feel worse than ever, she told me she was tired and sick of Cal and wished herself at home, Mrs Davis was in yesterday and said she was home sick, she has always stood up for the country but she says she is heartily sick of it, all her acquaintances are going home and she would like to go to. Capt Mann was in yesterday. I think he is hard up for he is cursing the country and he told me he could find nothing to do. Your father is sick with the headache. Sends much love to all and the baby in particular, he found a pair of Chinese shoes for her but there is not chance to send this time. I must give Bettie a line kiss baby for us and give love to all Mother and Horaces family.

Mother

SAN FRANCISCO, FEBY., 28 /53

{In T.L.M.'s hand}
Our Dear C.A.B.&J.,

Yours of Jan'y 16th arrived Feby. 19 & we can say it gives us equal pleasure to receive a letter by every mail from the states as it does you from Cal. I can assure you we were exceedingly anxious to hear from Angie, fearing she might have an ill turn, as it is quite apt to happen after so severe an sickness.

We would caution you to be prudent of your health. I do not mean to be shut up in your room but not be venturesome, always be careful to keep dry feet, because your mother can endure so much, is no certain guarantee for you. We are very anxious about you & you can hardly imagine how anxious we are to see the baby, Jennie Lewis- it appears sometimes our Jennie in Cal. would fly to Portland to kiss that very sweet little baby, what can't be beat, as C. says.

When Mrs. Robinson (she is now here) or Mrs. Calkin come in & call Jennie grandmother, you have no idea how Jennie starts up, & looks as young as a sweet eighteen—Well Bettie, if Grandmother was not with you this eve, what a fine time you would have chatting past events, we think it a happy thing you could be with Angie, in time of trouble, we feel under the greatest obligations for your kindness & hope some day to reward you in part.

John M. Sanford called on us the evening after we had mailed our letters, & said he would take a small bundle to states if we wished, having bought you a watch some week or two before concluded to send it & did so. He was to send it from Boston by express. It is a full jeweled leaver watch, the chain weighs $40. It should be used careful & never opened unless it is necessary. I shall expect a long letter on its reception from you.

I should have sent Arthur a present at the same time if I had purchased it, intend to send one at the first opportunity. He may be making a visit in Portland on the arrival of this. Make his visit as pleasant as possible. John, we are very anxious you should be doing something towards a livelyhood for the future.

As to the Farm. I think of but little more to say than to have what was said in my last letter carried out. I think it would be well to set out early in the spring those acacias, commencing near the gateway that leads to the barn, running on the bank as far as it is finished, setting them thirty inches from the inner edge of the face wall & one foot apart on a strait line, it may be well to set two near together like this .. .. If the season should be dry be sure to have them watered. Charles, if a yoke of oxen is needed on the farm, have them. be sure to have good, sound, healthy ones. John had better go to the farm after Morrill returns & see that all the tools are safe & put away all that are not needed. In describing the farming tools in my other letter I think I forgot the scraper, drag,

& wheelbarrow. All should be and probably are, carefully housed. It is my impression the timber, that is piled up in the field should be seen to, as soon as the snow is off, perhaps stack & covered over. Mr. Daniel Howard can tell you, it should not be neglected.

{In M.J.M.'s hand}
My dear Children[20]
   Yesterday I was going to write you a long letter as it was Sunday I thought I should not be disturbed. Mr. P. Clark took dinner with us, then Mr. Sewall Benson came in and we sat until tea time talking over old affairs and I laughed [until] I nearly split my sides at the anecdotes [they] related of Turner people. Then the evening [I thought I should] surely devote to you, but no, I must still [entertain] company until half past nine when I [thought] I would give it up and begin bright and [early when] through washing and then what a chance [I should] have but I have had calls the live long day- did not get through until dark and now a gentlemen waiting to play euchre. I [went] and priced some sleevelets for the baby and [was] to send them by this mail but I have [now] to go out and get them. I know you are _____ but it is a fact and I cannot make it otherwise. Your father has bought Arthur a splendid [set of] chess men but I do not know when we [shall have] a chance to send, I am almost dragged [out] and when my lady boarder leaves I am going [into the] country to stay one week with Mrs. Davis. The ladies are all well and always inquire for you. Give love to all. Tell Mary I saw Dr. Sturtevant and he is a perfect bloat, his eyes bursting from their sockets and his skin a red as a gooses foot. I do regret that I cannot say more. Tell the boys I am very impatient to see them little Arthur writes such truthful letters, so full of innocence that I can but weep over them Love to all in haste from
Your Father & Mother

---

20. A piece is cut out of this letter resulting in some blanks and conjectures. [1993]

My dear Children

Yours of the 16th, came safe to hand. The cigar case suited to a dot, the bonnet ribbon was very pretty, the one for the neck was beautiful, and the collar likewise, and I saw one in the shop window I thought would please you and I priced it, only eight dollars, but as I had bought you something so late, I thought Jennie must come next therefore I bought her some little shoulder knots, but I am bound to have the collar yet some day as I know it would suit your ladyship so well, it is of beautiful Honiton lace such as the Queen of England wore on her weding day. Uncle Horace is still here, he left here about four weeks since he said he was going to have a farm and raise a crop of potatoes or he was a dead man, he was going to Drakes bay just outside about thirty miles took an open boat with a ninny for a captain run on to a bar it being dark, they expected to be lost, they threw the seed potatoes overboard. Horace took off his clothes to swim ashore if he should be washed off, then clung to the mast with his flaps flying in the wind which he said was a signal of distress. John Q, says some one told him that when the day broke they found they were not more than four feet from the shore but Horace says it was no joke, he is the most like father of any of the brothers. Since I have been writing this Capt Mann came in said he had lost his ship, he undertook to take an old ship to Panama for a storeship for coal for the steam ship company, he got about four hundred miles from here he found she was sinking he hailed a ship and they took them all off and brought them back here, he feels mighty bad and the ship went down to see Davy Jones. We do feel quite uneasy about John but I do not know what is best, I think if you look at the date of the last letter I wrote him you will find that I was writing him at the same time that you were writing me on the same subject—I thought it quite singular. You spoke of the blue apron I have sent one with the box but you must do as you please about giving it to your friend.

My family are back again excepting Mr. Johnson and wife, they are housekeeping I expect she eats too many of my good greens as there seems to be quite a change coming over her.

The china boy is still here but as ugly as sin, he pinches my cat, and dog, you know nothing troubles me more than to have my pets abused. My health is not the best yet but I hope to get over it soon, but I assure you I have not been eating greens quite the opposite and your father tells me if I do not keep still I shall have to be upon my back for a year or two, that is a very pleasant prospect for me.

You know not how happy we all are to hear of the safty of some of the passengers [of the] Independence,[21] although there is many lost it is a relief to know where and how they died, What has become of Aunt Hannah? I think of her much, and Horaces family, in imagination, you and me go up to Turner and with little Jennie mount that capacious waggon and make a nice excursion around the country, visit the Tuttle farm, Aunt Nancy, and Mr. Pratts, and I am often at a stand what we shall do with ourselves when Grandmother is having a female prayer meeting at her house, I will leave it for you to decide. Say to your Charles I am very much obliged to him for his trouble in selecting the present and would be glad to make him a present but as he is not pleased with trifles I do not know what to select but he will enjoy looking at yours if you should be so fortunate as to receive it and any thing for Jennie he will enjoy anyway.

Give love to Bettie, say I would be most happy to write her but I could say nothing new and it is as much for her benefit as any and I expect she and I shall have some words to see who shall tend the baby.

Love to Aunts family tell them I see their cousins every week we walked out in the country the other day, took some crackers along and went where they were milking and had some crackers and milk.

I must leave do the best you can with John and leave the event. I hope all will be well

Your Mother

The Dr. has written his Aunt and wishes you to forward.

---

21. The *Independence* was a Vanderbilt steamer, sailing from San Juan to San Francisco. At daylight on February 16, 1852, she struck a sunken reef about a mile from the shore of the island of Santa Margarita, off the coast of Lower California. The vessel was beached in a little cove on the island but caught fire and in the resultant panic some 200 of the 414 passengers and crew lost their lives. See the *Annals of San Francisco*, p. 436.

My dear Children

A tax of a weekly mail has been imposed upon us, and I cannot like the idea of a mail coming without some news of home. I therefore will try to do as I would be done by. Yours of March 2nd was received and read many times over it brings you very near to read your letters, and the baby what a pity that I cannot be there to relieve you of the task of dressing. I cannot realize that I am not to be with you on my return, when I think of it seriously, I dread to go home, and find one link of our circle absent from our fireside.

Bettie writes me from W[inthrop] saying that John thought of staying at the farm if he will not spend his time foolishly I think it would be a fine thing, he is old enough to keep things in good shape, and it would be much pleasanter paying him than one who was looking out for themselves rather than his employers. Your father is very much afraid that he will get into bad company having no one to look after him, you must keep your eye upon him and give us a full account of him.

Uncle Horace is sitting by and thinking of home, he was interested in the steamer that was burnt on Missippi, he gave Lyman power of Attorney to sell some property, Lyman wrote him that he had done so, and invested the same in lard shipped on the Martha Washington, the next news was that she was burnt, but he would send him the insurance as soon as he could collect it, but not one word since, nor any money, he has written Lyman repeatedly but no answer, he asked me if you said any thing of the affair but I suppose you did not know any of the particulars, they are having fine times at their circle in Winthrop. I am right glad to hear they are enjoying themselves so much but I have seen so much of things a little more exciting I fear I shall never feel perfectly satisfied with their quiet ways again. Here you can step out of your house and see the whole world spread out before you in every shape and form. Your ears are filled with the most delightful music, your eyes are dazzeled with every thing that is beautiful, the streets are crowded the whole city are in the street. We have near us a splendid ice cream saloon which surpasses any thing I have seen in the states, very large windows with magnificent buff silk damask curtains with lace like those that Newhall Sturtevant boasts so much of, two large rooms are connected by an arch hung with the same material marble tables, floors and counters and as light as day at all hours of the night, The homeliest man in the city treated me to an ice cream there a few nights since at one dollar a glass.

I was up at Mrs Robinson last night, the Dr said he was coming down to get some medicine for his wife, she was sick at her stomach in the morning. I told him it was enough to make any woman sick to sleep with him. Little Charlie had on a red woolen shirt with blue drilling pants, she would not have thought once that it would have done to dress the little darling in that way.

I was in at Mrs Calkins today, all well, she and Mrs. Davis are making dresses all the while, I presume they have twenty five in a year a silk dress lasts but two months at the best. I know not why it is, but every thing goes to destruction in a very short time here. I wish you could be here a short time. it is so pleasant to have a plenty of money, we cannot seem to get a thousand together but if I want ten or twenty it is always ready, that will be another trouble when I get home, when I want five dollars to go to P[ortland], it will be hard work to raise it. I have been making me a brown silk, and next week I am going to make me a black one, to day I have been making a pink thibet sack trimmed with velvet ribbon but I am sure I do not know when I will wear it. I shall send you some pieces of them by Mr. Adams who has promised to take a package for me, he goes in May I had a line from Artie one page just the same number of lines and sentences in every one. Give abundance of love to him and Charlie, Bettie, Johny and all the Aunts, cousins and the Turner folks.

Mother

Your father and uncle send love.

My dear Angie

We are going to send an old steamer with a weekly mail, and I shall not make a great effort to make it interesting as it will not probably reach you before the one that starts the first of May.

I will begin with telling you of my domestic trials, My China boy was so ugly that I could do nothing with him, it was so unlike any thing we have with us. I will cite a few instances, I had some ladies call upon me one afternoon when the wind was blowing a gale, he ran down, opened the front [door] and fastened it with the mat, I told him to shut it, but I had to say it quite a number of time before he would start, then he slammed it with the mat in between the door and frame. I took a raw hide your father bought for the purpose and laid it onto his back a few times but he looked as though he would have killed me if he dared, he drove a nail into the tea kettle, he would knock the noses off the pitcher against the fosset of the water barrel, put grease on the stove to make a smoke and laugh when I scolded him: he would come up behind me and stick burning matches under my nose, then he would take every opportunity to annoy my cat and dog, he took great pains to slop my floor after I had cleaned it, if I chanced to have a clean cloth on the table, he would put all the slops in a cup and tip it over, the Dr asked him why he did it, he said, more money, We thought it best to let him go and we have now a small French boy but he knows nothing of the kitchen and it makes my work very hard, but to day I flew around, and got my work done in season to dress in my pink thibet sack, and they complimented me very highly on my good looks, if I had some good teeth I should look as good as new.

Yesterday I had two ladies to spend the day and last evening Annie Webb and her brother and wife - she is a sister of E. Merrills wife she was quite astonished to find so many comforts here. I treated her to a piece of mince pie, which she said was excellent.

Dr Robinson and wife took me to the theatre this week, all dead heads, as the Dr still composes comic songs and sings them, for fifteen dollars a night.

The play was green bushes, or one hundred years ago, the after piece was, a kiss in the dark; where all jealous husbands ought to have been.

Mrs. Davis was in to day. She is very well. Tell Mary her friends are well.

I want you to write me when you do not receive our letters. How many mails have missed taking some word to you for us.

There is three gentlemen sitting here telling me it is all nonesense writing every week. of course I must stop. Remember me to all especially Charles Bettie and the boys and the dear little baby kiss for your Mother

SAN FRANCISCO SATURDAY, MAY 7TH/53

Dear C. & Angie,

Your letter dated April 3d & one from John & Arthur, were received in due time & with much interest. The baby you say much about, & so you ought, you can now know the anxiety of parents. We have no doubt Jennie is one of the finest babies that is & you can hardly imagine our anxiety to see it & you all. John told us about the farm, we are in hopes now to hear regular semi-monthly, how it is getting along, with all the particulars, you will please urge him to write every two weeks.

We shall expect occasionally some general news of the farm, from Charles. Who is the hired man to work with John? how near my plan is carried out &c, do not fail to have that part of the pasture next to Towles plowed and sowed to oats. I wrote John a long letter giving him caution not to be too ambitious, but work steady. I hope he will have a good man with him.

Angie, I wish you to send John a good Dictionary & tell him not to write without being very certain every word to correct, if this method is pursued, he cannot fail to have his letters instructive to himself & interesting to us. Charles, we are about building commence next week. We think it better than pay rent. Jennie will give you more particulars in her next. Shall send money by the steamer of the 15th to take up the railroad bond that Capt. Clark holds. Thank Bettie for her kind letter & tell Charles to give her a good kiss for me. Love to all. Please let us know in your next if you have received all letters from us. We write every mail. In haste and with much love from your father T.L.M.

My dear Angie
Sunday after dinner, your father on the bed with the headache the family all out.

I would like to tell you something that would interest you, during the week between the mails I think of many things to say to you but when the time arrives it leaves without a trace.

We have at last settled our business, and last week there was some prospect of my going home. A gentleman offered a fair sum for our lot on conditions that he could buy this of Plume, but he would not sell, thinking he could rent to us and be sure of his pay but he is mistaken, Your father has thought it best to build slightly. They began the house yesterday are to have it completed in ten days, Some fun in having a house completed in a fortnight. Had he sold I should have gone home, if your father concluded to stop and let his money, as it is bringing high rates of interest here now, it would bring two or three hundred per month, what at home it would only bring that in a year,

If it were not for John, I would not be in haste to go home, as it is much better that Arthur should keep along with his studies and you I feel quite at rest about as far as your bodily wants are concerned and Bettie has a chance with you if she wishes it. I do hope Albion will get him a situation in a shop as it is quite necessary he should have a trade if he does not get it these five years, I fear he will get tired of the farm and it will be no better than when he began, although he is abundantly able to do well.

I think it is quite singular that you and I should be writing about the same thing at nearly the same time, you said you would like a box to be sent around the Horn. I think we sent it but a short time before. There are not many curiosities in it, but I think its contents will be acceptable, and I would be glad to send one by every ship that goes home, but somehow I do not come across anything as yet. I called on a lady last week who had a present of a case of insects from China it was beautiful, they had a needle put through their bodies and stuck into the wood which kept them in place, with glass over them, they were so arranged with their different colors that at a little distance, it looked like a picture. I thought of you, and if possible I shall get one but I have never seen one as pretty as that, in the city.

Philo Clark came in town to day and brought me a fine boquet, I know you would laugh at the idea of three large thistle for the centre of a boquet surrounded with what we call at home, butter and eggs, intermixed with a bright scarlet flower something like our London Pride, but I think it much prettier than none; he brought a few oysters and I made a stew for our tea, they were taken from Oregon and put into a creek but they do not flourish in this region.

Uncle Horace is still here, like Mr Macawber waiting for something to turn up, he had four great projects in view, one is the conquest of Jappan dont laugh, it is true that he has made quite an effort to get a clipper ship have every man put in a certain sum and go in for the chances of making a fortune by trading peacably if they would, if not try the effect of a little more grape; Another is taking Sonora a country lying on the gulf of Cal. which he says has in some parts been deserted on account of the Apache Indians being so troublesome he thinks fifty men with a good rifle and a pair of Colts revolvers could drive the whole race.[22] The third is the application of Ericsons steam power for agricultural purposes. The fourth and last is marrying a fortune he says he wants something to love, he will probably know the result before long, he says what little progress he has made has kept him from many dissapations.

---

22. Various filibustering ventures from California, including the Pindray, Raousset-Boulbon, Walker, and Crabb expeditions found otherwise.

Poor Mother I know very well how much she feels for her absent child and I would be right glad to be with her but I cannot bear the idea of being obliged to earn a living in the states. The Dr. wrote father a long letter and is waiting patiently for an answer. Give much love to all the Turner friends. I should think some of Horaces family might write me for the sake of an answer if they do not care to gratify me. I should like much to hear how they are situated at their new home.

Kate Hayes has sung her last song in Cal in singing the Irish Emigrants lament, her heart was too full and she was obliged to retire, some say it was for effect, others that she was sincere but she had a fine house, and was escorted to the Hotel by the firemen where they gave her three cheers and parted well satisfied on all sides. Mrs Sinclair is creating some excitement in the theatrical world, but it is merely curiosity to see one of whom there has been so much said, I saw her in the play of the Stranger, her part was one which she could play from experience but I do not think much of her as an actress, although she is very fine looking but I think her race is not long here as a popular actress.[23]

The ladies of your acquaintance here are very well and always ask for Angie and the baby, I hope I have a picture soon. Say to Mary her cousins were here and spent the day last week had a great time telling stories. Mrs. Hubbard is coming home next spring with us but Mrs. Drew has not got through the honeymoon yet; she thinks it delightful.

And now for the baby, I am delighted with your praises of her, I hope they will not abate as there is a gentleman boarding here, who has had a little sister since he left and they write almost the

---

23. Catherine Sinclair, actress-manager of the newly erected Metropolitan Theater, and former wife of the famous actor, Edwin Forrest. After divorce from her jealous and vindictive husband, Mrs. Sinclair won recognition as an actress in her own right in New York before she came to California. After playing in San Francisco and Sacramento, she opened the Metropolitan on Christmas Eve, 1853, as Lady Teazle in *The School for Scandal*. Edwin Booth was a member of the cast. The play was an outstanding event in San Francisco theatrical history. Mrs. Megquier made her unfavorable comment when Mrs. Sinclair first appeared in San Francisco.

same of her word, for word, that you do of Jennie, and do not want he should get ahead. I hope you have received the ties and she must have them on every day. I hope you will keep her posted about her grandparents. How I would like to squeeze her. I have often thought of Mrs Hopkins give love to her say that we feel grateful for her kindness to you. And now good wishes to Charlie, Angie, Bettie, Johnie, Artie and Jennie.

Your father will write Charles

With much love Mother

Charles I enclose a draft of $800 for you to take up a railroad bond that Capt. Clark took from me. It may require $50. more. Please take it up immediately & keep it in your hands, collect the interest semi-annually & make use of it you think best. Write all about the farm.

Yors affect'y   T.L.M.

SAN FRANCISCO MAY 31 / 53

My dear Children

It is but one word that I can say to you for we have been moving to day and you well know what a muss we are in for the first twelve hours and I have got my meals the same as though nothing had been doing. We have got a snug little tenement and it will seem much better than paying one hundred per month for house rent, your father is almost tired to death, and the kitty is very much frightened but I am as good as new. O that you could look in upon us this eve, You said the picture was a good one, but did not say how you sent it, and we have not been able to find it, but we supposed by mail, and your father went and stood in the line of expectancy twice for an hour but no picture of the dear baby. I was so disappointed that I spoiled my work that I was cutting, but I shall look with impatience until the next mail the gentlemen inquire every day if the baby has come yet- I heard by the way of P. Clarks wife of Turner that they heard I was sick, do tell them I

LOLA HAS COME!

am as well as ever in my life. You say that you are preparing for our return. I shall come if we can rent to good advantage but your father will not come to Maine again in cold weather.

Lola Montes is making quite a stir here now but many say that her playing is of that character that it is not proper for respectable ladies to attend but I do want to see her very much. Mr Clark said in dancing the spider dance a favorite play of hers where she performs the antics of one with a tarantula upon their person and some thought she was obliged to look rather higher than was proper in so public a place.[24]

---

24. Marie Dolores Eliza Rosanna Gilbert, the Lola Montez of later years, was born in Limerick, Ireland, in 1818. A girl of many affairs, wanderings, and vicissitudes, she finally so infatuated Kid Ludwig I of Bavaria that he built her a palatial villa, made her the countess of Landsfeld, supplied her with money, and at last abdicated under popular pressure as a result of his extravagances and indiscretions.

I am anxiously looking for Betties fashions. We had a long letter from Moses B giving the Winthrop news but it given in so scientific manner that it lost a part of its interest to me. Your father sent a draft to take up the railroad bond that Mr. Clark held and he wishes Charles to look after likewise a ministerial tax if there is one.

I hope to hear from John and Artie next mail you I look upon as sure.

Give love to all our friends. What does Grandpa Gilson say to the baby give love to them and know that we shall be with you as soon as possible

Your mother

San Francisco June 15/53

Our dear Angie & Charles,

We have the unpleasant word to say, that long wished for picture has not come, neither did we have any letters by the last mail. We think some muss is about being stirred up, for one year we have not failed before of having our letters regular.

In 1851 Lola came to America but met with only mediocre success on the stage until in the spring of 1853 she reached San Francisco. Her fame, colored and magnified by skilled publicity that even Hollywood might envy, assured her an overwhelming reception. She was the "divine Lola," the "incarnation of brave wickedness and splendid folly," the nymph of many lovers "who bathes in lavender water and dries herself with rose leaves." In truth, as George R. MacMinn well says, "Lola Montez was not so much a factual person as a living legend.

Lola played in the American Theatre, for a time attracting the "most brilliant and overflowing audiences" that San Francisco had ever known. Her greatest triumphs were achieved in the play, *Charlotte Corday,* written especially for her, and in the vivid, frenzied, highly sensation dance, *La Tarantella.* See illustration, p. 128.

After some weeks of glory, Lola was burlesqued and perhaps driven off the stage by the Megquier's friend, Dr. D.G. Robinson, and Catherine Chapman, "the darling of San Francisco." On July 3, 1853, Lola married Patrick P. Hull and temporarily retired from the theater. She appeared again on the San Francisco stage in the fall of 1856 and gave a farewell performance in mid-October at the Metropolitan just before she left California, never to return. She died in New York, January 17, 1861, in obscurity and want—and perhaps in piety.

Your Mother, as well as myself have been in high fever ever since your letter stating the baby was coming, you can have no idea how many restless nights we have had in consequence.

We built a house, 26 by 50, in ten days & moved in the last day of May, as we wrote.

I write Arthur by this mail & sent him a plan of the house, wishing him to draw it off & send you & John one or send the original. It is a true design—Jennie, with her cousin John Q. has gone to ride, started ½ past two o'clock will return at 6. I am now keeping house, have had two callers. They were nearly tired out, been house hunting, was obliged to give them a little stimulus & doughnuts—having been hindered sometime by callers I shall be obliged to close & see to the fire, please tell me how the farm is moving along give the particulars in your next. Jennie will give you the news—adieu In haste from your father

{In M.J.M.'s hand}

We have had a nice ride, found all the gentlemen waiting for tea which was put on in a short space, and I have an hour to devote to you. I do feel quite homesick when a whole month passes without one word from you and the picture I cannot be reconciled to the loss of it.

Duelling is now the order of the day, there has been three, and there was three more on the eve of coming off when one the parties shot, died, a fine young man of twenty two and it seems to have cooled their blood considerably and nothing has been said of them too day. The weather is excessively hot for San Francisco. I think it makes the people fractious. I hope you will not think me getting fond of dissapation because I write you of the plays. I went to a benefit given Dr Robinson, there was a perfect jam, the actors and actresses volunteered their services and the proceeds amounted to one thousand dollars, we had first, The school for scandal then a song, two acts of Richard 3rd, a dance from Master and Miss Chapmans, a song from the Dr himself setting up Lola, then the loan of a lover, everyone seemed delighted, he was cheered loudly every time he followed himself whether on the stage of off.[25] Lola Montes has given two benefits one to the firemen one to the Hebrew benevolent society each of them over three thousand.

The grain is getting quite yellow and the grass is getting dry while with you every thing is beautiful, I do want to see it and if I live shall another spring, whether your father comes or no, he thinks property is rising, it certainly is astonishing to see the building that is going on in the city, I do certainly dread our quiet house but still my thoughts are ever with you and I shall have much less care of which I am tired but I know there is no other way at present.

I do feel disappointed in not getting Betties letter of fashions. I shall wait until they come before I start out on another dress I mean if it comes next mail.

My ears are greeted with the most delightful music. I think the firemen are out. I do wish you could hear it, I do feel so anxious about John. I imagine him alone on the farm thinking of his absent friends. Is it not cruel that we must be away. Not one word from you, Charles, do write all of you. And the dear little Jennie. I image her sitting on the floor playing with Betties work basket, but I must leave you with a world of good wishes to all who would accept them.

Your mother

SAN FRANCISCO JUNE 15/53

To Our Affect. Son Arthur,

Not having received a letter by the last mail from anyone, is to us, quite odd, & very singular, we cannot think the fault is our children, we have been very fortunate in our letters, only one failure for the past year, of having a letter from one or all, by every mail—

---

25. Such benefits were a universal custom for popular actors or singers in San Francisco. The Chapman family were extremely popular on the stage in San Francisco and at the mines, and Caroline Chapman won especial applause in her burlesque of Lola Montez. In later years, however, the city turned against these burlesques and restored Lola to high favor.

We hope you had the pleasure of seeing Mr. Adams, being direct from us, as he will hand you a few small presents from us, & it is quite probable the trinkets we sent you around the horn, will arrive near the time of this letter, you will then see some of the Chinese ingenuity in cutting ivory &c.

Arthur we intended to have answered your request to spend the haying season on the farm, in the affirmative, & I can assure you we felt very unpleasant about it, we were in hopes Angie would see that your wishes were gratified. The reason of our neglect was we were about moving in our new house that we were building at that time.

I will give you a plan of it on another piece of paper,[26] our house joins the one (Richmond house) we have been living in for the last ten months— We are much pleased with the change, it is more convenient & not upstairs, our family continues the same, except Tiger, he was sick & some of our boarders gave him away, & your mother has one of finest & most inteligent cat in all California, she has to be tended & cooed over certainly twice per day, always answers when spoken to & can nearly talk. We are very anxious to have a line from you giving a description of your vacation, how you are pleased with the baby &c. We hope you are enjoying yourself as much as possible, under the circumstances, give Mr. & Mrs. Abbot our best regards, together with your school fellows & accept of this from your Father.

Dear Arthur I can only say how much we want to see you and I presume at your age you can see no reason for our staying so long but it is not pleasant to be poor, and we do hope to [be] able to be with you soon but we could not have given you an education so you must submit to some inconvenience to be fitted for after life but the time passes swiftly and if we all live we shall soon be again together. I have to lavish my affection upon my kitten and she

---

26. The one-story wooden building was on 139 Jackson Street. It was 26 feet wide and about 50 feet deep. The store in the front took up half the space; two bedrooms, a sitting room, dining room, cook room, and store room made up the rest. [1993]

returns it four fold she is now running around the house and wants to get in my lap- but she plays with my pen and it wont do.

I hope you will have a good time on the farm. Make hay when the sun shines is the wish of your mother.

SAN FRANCISCO, JULY 31, [1853][27]

Dear daughter

Your letter and presents came safely to hand, and as good luck would have it I was dressed for dinner when your Father brought them in, I clapped them on in two seconds after their arrival, in the evening there was a ball and [I] wore the rest, so you perceive I do not allow anything to lay by to get yellow, they were a perfect Godsend. I do not know how I should have done without them.

We have rented our house, so much towards getting ready to return, but do not be too much elated for that is but a small part of what we have got to do before we can leave, we disposed of all our household furniture which consisted of various things, namely, and we were boarding with a family from New Bedford, there are four ladies of us and we have some nice times.

We were very sorry that Arthur did not go with John as he is getting old enough to improve fast, and in Turner he can do nothing to improve his mind. I think it a fine place to keep fat, but nothing more. I am very glad you have got his wardrobe in order. I think you will be so well educated in that office that I shall not resume it on my return. The Winthrop folks have not arrived they took a sailing vessel from Panama will probably be here the last of August. Uncle Daniel Haywards brother, Alvan, from western New York brought us the news, he arrived in the steamer before the last and returns in this steamer sick of Cal. He thinks those that have homes in the states had better stay where they are which is the opinion of nearly every one on their arrival but if they are successful it changes

---

27. Some time in the fall of 1853, Mary Jane Megquier returned to Portland without her husband who stayed behind trying to secure his claim on Cyrus Richmond's estate. [1993]

the aspect of affairs materially. I do not see why Horace or his wife cannot give me a line. I should like exceedingly to hear from them. I wish you would buy the children a nice dress each, a thibet or something that will be of service as a present from their Aunt Jane, if we are successful in getting our property home I shall make Horace a present but every thing is so uncertain that we can make no calculations for the future. I hope that Cousin Charles [Haskell] will remunerate himself for all his trouble and you must see that he does, and Cousin Mary must not be forgotten, likewise the Grandmother. It is my most ardent wish that Grandmother P[ollard] may be spared that I may look upon her once more. I am very sorry it is so dull in W[inthrop] for I still have quite an attachment to its beautiful lakes and hills and the inhabitants are not the worst although they are given to gossip a very little. But it is not to be wondered at where there is so little to take up ones attention.

Capt Mann is still here in the harbor doing nothing, says he is expecting a friend here who will buy a ship for him and then he will make his fortune. Mr. Calkin is here doing nothing in very low spirits. He seems to have lost his ambition, he is one of the unfortunate as yet— he wants very much to get his family here but I am sure I do not know what he would do with them. Mr. Davis is here he thinks he cannot stand it without Annah much longer but it is very bad crossing the isthmus or he would send for her immediately.

I must save a little for Mary and Betty as you have the reading you will not be particular to whom it is addressed. Write the boys and tell them they are ever in my mind.

Your Mother

Heard from Sam Barrett is well, but have heard from none of the brig Margaret boys

[SAN FRANCISCO MARCH ? 1854][28]

{In T.L.M.'s hand}
My dear Daughter

Your beautiful letter of Jan. 15th was received in due time, but not feeling very well I did not feel like writing & you know if I do not write your Mother, she will be homesick & I fear leave you for Cal. It is true I should be very happy to see her, but for your and the boys sake I prefer to have her with you. I remain an old batch, very probably now, another year. I can assure you it is not pleasant, the evenings are lonesome. Sabbaths, if well, I attend meeting, lately at Mr. P_____ at North beach, generally at Mr. Brierlys a

---

28. Thomas Megquier returned home some time in 1854 presumably in time to help supervise the building of a large white house on Bramhalls Hill. In December, 1854, he took out a mortgage of two thousand dollars on the property. Russell B. Norton to Thomas L. Megquier and Mary J. Megquier, 8 December 1854, Book 196, p. 458, Kennebec Country Registry of Deeds. [1993]

Baptist on Washington Street, he, by the way, is one of the smartest men we have. In this country they say very little about the doctrine. They have quite enough to do to keep their morals in tune.

You say your Mother talks of going to housekeeping soon. I wrote her some time since, I thought she had better stay with you till April or late in the spring, as there could not be much done on the farm till then & I had strong fears she and Arthur going from a warm house to a barn would get sick. You must advise them. Your Mother I understand intends trying her skill in building a house this season. I expect it will be something nice, don't you? I am thinking I shall have a finger in the pie after all. That plan I sent her the first of Feby. has no doubt arrived by this time. Then there is another in the box of presents gone around the horn, will probably arrive in April, then you can have one to look at. Angie, you must go to the farm this summer & spend a little of your taste in laying out the grounds, & see that the hedge is well arranged & plan carried out. I would like to have it look rather nicer than Miss Leavetts—I think it could be done with a little time & perserverance. The Major will have something to say in her case, though I understand they are not to be married till after their house is finished. I shall expect when you go to Winthrop, to have a description of their premises from you.

Angie I am very anxious about your health. I hardly can see why you are so feeble, do tell me what appears to be the greatest difficulty, was it nursing the baby or anything that occurred at confinement, do take good care of yourself, I know you have one of the kindest of husbands & there can be nothing wanting there. The picture that was sent of our group at home was fine, beautiful, as natural as life.[29] Your friend that saw it here thought you rather handsome. I did not dispute them. Little Jennie a little darling. What pleasure it would give me to see her, it would be one of the happiest moments of my life. But if my life and health is spared me & that too of my dear family at home, a year will soon pass away &

---

29. See photograph of Mary Jane Megquier with Arthur and John and Charles, Angie, and Jennie Gilson on page 134. [1993]

bring us together once more which is the sincere prayer of your father— Angie while writing your letter I was called to a case of Obs., a young lady 20 years old & about as tall as Bettie, much fleshier, was there about eight hours, the boy weighed 9 lbs- doing well. Hannah Davis expects to be confined in April and so does Mrs. Lord. You spoke of Hattie True. I am very sorry for their misfortunes. Give her & family & Mary my best regards & the same to Aunt Reynolds, Mary & her hus.

CHAPTER THREE

THIRD JOURNEY

San Francisco
November 1855 to June 1856
Mary Jane Megquier

NOV. 4TH, 55

My dear Angie

After the usual amount of hardships which seem my fortune to encounter, I am at last in the good city of San Francisco.[1] I would be most happy to give you a true and impartial account of my journey but it would be but a repetition of what has been so many times written, it would not astonish, it could not fail to amuse you to listen [to] the anathamas pronounced upon the Nicaragua route. For my part there were much to interest. We were crowded on to a small steamer on the morning of the 30th of Sept. and made very good progress while all were delighted with the variety of scenery that presented itself but when nature called for a seat and something for stomach then came the curses on the transit route, but we managed to have any amount of fun Mr. Johnson, Emily and myself, with the help of a few others made the best of it. We managed to get a small bit of tongue, hard bread with the nice cake gave us a comfortable meal, yet there were many that I would have been glad to have shared with us yet size would not admit. One lady had the good fortune to have

---

1. Mary Jane Megquier returned to San Francisco hoping to settle the claim on Richmond's estate. Thomas remained in Maine where he was ill. [1993]

some tea and a pot, which soon gained the name of the infuriated tea pot it was in such requisition.

We arrived at Castella rapids at two oclock in the morning when all rushed ashore anticapating the pleasure of breakfasting[2] upon broiled chicken and fresh eggs but there new disappointments awaited us, the country was invaded by fillibusters which had cut off all supplies and we were obliged to make the best of stewed pork half cooked beans, musty bread and tea that would make you shudder like the bitterest herb.[3] After growling and cursing we at last were transferred to a fine steamer on lake Nicaragua arrived at Virgin bay at sunset the wind blowing a perfect gale which made it very interesting to land eight hundred in an open boat about a mile from shore, women and children screaming expecting every moment would be their last, but we were all at last safely landed into the miserable town at the head of Virgin bay where some were obliged to pay as high as fifteen dollars for a chance to lay their heads but the next day we got orders on the steamship company for our expenses as we were to be detained a week. We spent three days very pleasantly although all were nearly starved for the want of wholesome food but you know my stomach is not lined with pink satin, the bristles on the pork, the weavels in the rice and worms in the bread did not start me at all, but grew fat upon it all. Emily, Miss Bartlett and myself had a small room with scarce light enough to see the rats and spiders we had to lay crosswise the bed to give us room, we would let our feet hang over the bead until the circulation became torpid then we would draw them up until all was right again.

We were there three days when we packed ourselves into a miserable waggon with four of the most dilappated animals at-

---

2. See the illustration on page 142.
3. This was the period of William Walker's activities in Nicaragua. Walker, a native of Tennessee, came to California in 1850 and three years later led an abortive filibustering expedition to effect the "independence" of Lower California and Sonora. In 1855 Walker took a company of "emigrants" to Nicaragua and the next year seized the presidency of the country. Four years later, after incurring the enmity of Cornelius Vanderbilt, he was executed by a firing squad at Trujillo.

tached, fourteen of our party inside, with a basket of crackers a few bottles of claret, made our exit after waiting two hours for the arrangements to be completed and arrived on the shores of the Pacific after walking two miles in a beautiful shower, which you well know is not unpleasant for me at four in the afternoon. As the transit company had our expenses to pay they hurried us on board the steamer where they were coaling and the utmost state of confusion prevailed so many crowded on to a steamer only half large enough to accomadate the number of passengers. One lady died in a few hours with the cholera which made everyone . . .

{End of sheet; remainder of letter evidently lost}

{Marginal note}

Give love to Arthur and tell him I shall write as soon as I get time.

SAN FRANCISCO NOV 29TH /55

My dearest Angie

It is Thanksgiving and all alone so I will devote a part of the day to you, as I cannot be with you. Nothing would give me more pleasure than to look upon my dear children but if I must submit to what I have for some time past, I shall never see you again in Maine, but I have not a doubt but I shall be with you at some day not far distant. The very air I breathe seems so very free that I have not the least desire to return. I do long for the time when I can sell the property and send some money home for I know how very much it is needed but I can do nothing until the return of the paper that was sent last mail. Emily has gone to the Ocean House, about eight miles from the city. She says she is very unhappy but to me she seems as happy as most women, for she has much sympathy, and no doubt receive much more attention than if nothing had happened.

Her husband was here an evening or two since for the first time for three weeks, he is very anxious to be divorced but she wishes to hear from her brothers before using any active measures.

BREAKFASTING ON SHORE, NICARAGUA LAKE, 1853.

There is to be a wedding on the opposite side of the street to
night one of the belles of the city. it will take place in church, all
the town are to be there to see the bride, I would like to see her to
tell you of her, She has eyes black as any dolls hair of the same hue,
quite small in stature, skin like wax, but I think she is not burdened
with more than one idea at a time. The Allies had a great dinner to
celebrate the fall of Sebastopol but the only demonstration I saw
was any quantity of them most essentially corned[4] Mrs. Robinson
always inquires for you her husband is in the mines, her brother is
with her here, she is as good as ever. Mrs. Davis is the same situation
that you were one year ago her little girl reminds me of Jennie but
she is much handsomer I think I never saw one so pretty. Mrs.
Calkin is the same, they with Mrs. Clapp were here to lunch last
week, but I had so many calls I could not prevail on them to stay.

---

4. The fall of Sebastopol, an incident in the Crimean War, occurred September 20, 1855.

Counting them up when we retired there were twenty-three quite as many as we could entertain to advantage.

Say to Jennie I had some music from a handorgan, there was a little monkey with a red coat trimmed with button, a little straw hat which he held out to every passer by for a shilling, I went to housekeeping for the sake of making a house for Emily where there would not be quite as many looking at her as at the Hotel but I think she now likes the excitement as well as myself every one is astonished that her husband can treat her so. They say she would be picked up in a short time if she were free. You can have no idea of the attention she receives. I think she will be loath to leave the country if her brothers think it best.

Uncle Horace is still without any visible means of support but looks as though he lived on the fat of the land and as full of fun as ever, Every one is pleased with him, it would only take a good suit of clothes to take him into the best society, if I were able I would take care of him for his company, He is ever negotiating, you would think he done more business than any man in the city. Mr Snell calls but his business is anything but flourishing. I do not like to go into his store it looks so unlike what it did in former times. I began to tell you of my housekeeping but ran off on another subject, Mr Johnson who used to board with us and came on the steamer with us took a great interest in Mrs Barstow [Emily] and went househunting with her found one on the same street that I have ever lived on and she was so anxious that Johnson told me he would furnish me with funds if I would begin. So I took the house hoping to get a boarder or two enough to support myself but it is so far up town I have not found any yet, but Mr Gibson. I borrowed one hundred which you know goes but little ways, but I hope to have one to fill a vacant room which will just pay for the bread I eat, and rent, which is all I expect to do at present, but I assure you I have never for a moment regretted that I left Winthrop, that beautiful house has no charms for me at present, and should I know I would never visit it again, it would give me no sorrow if I should have the trials I have endured there,

BEECHCROFT, WINTHROP, ME, BUILT BY THE MEGQUIERS IN 1854 [1993].

DEC. 3D

My dear Angie,

Are you aware that your letter was written the day after the steamer sailed? Which accounts for my not hearing from you last mail. Mr. Jose wrote that your Father is very sick[5] if he should be taken away it will only be what I have wished that might come upon myself, rather than live with one who was ever wishing me to sacrifice my health to his gratification. I endured it, I thought as long as I could, I know what the world will think of me, but my regrets are that I have no money to send. But to Charles I would say get enough to pay the expenses for there is no doubt of my selling as soon as I get the power, and you shall have it with interest, but it is impossible to rent a wooden building when there are so many brick ones untenented, but it is a desirable location if there was a

---

5. Thomas L. Megquier died on November 8, 1855. [1993]

building upon it. I shall consult Mr. Burbank and know what measures to take (if the Dr. is unable to attend to it) before this leaves. I am sorry to trouble you for I know you have much to do, but I know of no one else to apply to. I hope to hear of the good health of yourself and children. If Charles is not well, go to Winthrop with the little ones and tell him to come here for dispepsia is unknown here.

Love to all and do the best you can, and know you are ever in your Mothers thought, how much my doings may prove to the contrary, kiss the babies, with the best of love of your

Mother

Dec. 9th. Mr. Burbank says if the Dr. cannot sign his name, you must send witnesses to that effect and appoint me, or someone else, guardian, if not living, use measures to authorize me to sell as the expenses must be paid. Charles you will attend to it, wont you? And send by the next mail after the receipt of this and oblige your mother

SAN FRANCISCO FEB 4TH [1856]

My dear Angie

Yours of the first of Jan arrived in due time and twice happy it made me to know you did not think me an indifferent wife and Mother, John says he thinks it best for me to come home, of course, I would not ask him to come if he thinks it best to stay, as there are many uncertainties connected with the journey which would fall heavy upon me should either of my friends be the victim. And now all I am to do is to sell as soon as the law will allow, as I am anxious to be square with the world, and place the boys above want, But for myself I do want to be with you, but if I am obliged to work hard for a living, I had rather do it here than home. I look to my home in Winthrop as my final home but not until I can procure for my children the reasonable comforts of life without intruding upon any ones generosity but my own. I know there are many happy days in store for us in that beautiful house where I often turn with an ardent wish to be there and nothing reconciles me but to look upon what I have suffered and should still unless I was independent. As it regards a slight from Miss Alice I look upon it as a blessing, for I could not ever be reconciled to any attachment in that quarter and therefore any neglect would prove a favor. While yourself with Charles, the little ones with John and Arthur and myself lives so dearly in the hearts of each other, I defy the world to give me one single pang in the shape of a slight for with the beauties of nature with that little society I can be as happy as the majority, if they do not choose to court our friendship. I wrote you last I was at Mrs. Robinsons where I am still, and she wishes me to stay while she is alone, and shall do so unless something offers where I can make a few scads.

I read what you said of her which gave her much pleasure, as she has but few friends in comparison with those who have plenty of money to make a great show in the world, but she is none the less worthy and her husbands prospects are very flattering now, but he seems to have been a victim for dame fortune to play her tricks upon. Charles Jose wrote to Emily I had represented things differently from what I should, I have said as little about her as I possibly could as it was her request for she seems to think her situation can be kept a secret and I do not know what I have said, but this I do know I have told truth when I said any thing, and had I time I would write to Charles for I have done my best to have her misfortune fall as lightly as possible upon her, and she has borne it nobly but still there is a wish that I cannot fathom to keep every thing a secret, as it respects her funds. I thought it honorable in her to try to support herself and did not know that she wished me to keep it to myself, and I told her I should disguise no truths to please any one, if they asked where she was I should tell them, and from the tenor of her letters from home, I know the truth is displeasing, therefore I will not write any thing more of her, only she is well and still with me.

There is a gentleman friend of Mrs. Robinsons who discourses Byron beautifully, visits her on Sunday night. I assure you we have an intellectual treat he is full of wit and last night it was midnight before the party broke up. Em. went to bed, Mrs. R's eyes were often shaded by those drooping lids but the brother and myself were ardent listeners. His opinion of church and the world are the same as mine therefore I listened with interest but there is nothing pleasing in his personal appearance.

Mr. Johnson of whom you often hear me speak is my gallant whenever I wish to go, he takes me to the mercantile lectures or any where I would like. I do not go to the theatres nor balls to both I am invited but decline. We do not have so many calls as when we were housekeeping. One reason it is a very bad place to get to on account of grading the streets, another they do not feel as much at home as in my house, but we are busy with our sewing in the day, our evenings are devoted to all sorts of games that can be got up, Charley which you no doubt remember is a stout boy and really a very smart one too. I asked him to draw a picture to send to Jennie, in ten minutes they were done without any effort on his but to put his pencil upon paper and let it slide.

The poetry is from the Doct [Robinson] who is always giving some one a hit. He writes beautiful letters to his wife, they have more wit and talent than can be often found, as he is so very steady I do not see why they may not some day take a high position.

I had a line from Bettie and Milton [Benjamin] both of which I must answer. Tell Charles it was a pleasure to look upon his writing. I took it to the lawyer and they said he was smart- they knew by his writing. I told them I was proud of him. I have seen them so much we are very familiar or they would not have taken that freedom to make remarks upon my friends. Jen and Scott[6] I see them now just making preparations to go to bed, as it is now just three o clock here. I would be glad to give them a kiss, but the time will soon pass. I have written Mother and shall write the boys. I think John had better have his fathers watch and sell his. The watch of mine I shall let remain until I get money to send the Doct, then I want the articles left with you until I come. Love to all and much to you and your family

Mother

----

6. The Gilsons' second child, Arthur Scott (1855–1914), was born before Mary Jane Megquier left for her third journey. The Gilsons' other children were: Henry Clinton (1857–1937), Anne (1863–1937), Charles (1871–93), and Marjary (1873–1967). [1993]

My dear Angie,

Yours of Jan 17th came to hand three days since, and papers likewise, and were it not that law compels me to stay for months or years I would be with you in one short month, but if you were here I should never wish to be in Maine again. The few words you told me that Mr Clark said, told too plainly what I should have to contend with in Winthrop and if nothing more I wish to be independent, then they can say what they please for with you and the boys I can be happy We are still with Mrs. Robinson and enjoying myself as well as possible, if I could only raise money to send home, I would rest easy for awhile, but it keeps me awake, thinking how the boys get along.

Business is dull indeed, the building is again vacated and if I cannot get more rent than I have, I shall fit it up and rent the rooms which will bring me more than I can get any other way, and will give me some employment to keep them in order[7] I am going to write Milton, and Mr. Clark, I think I can tell him some things that may shut his mouth but I shall not bring you into any muss but if I do not have enough to make me unhappy without any of my pretended friends speaking slightly of those I love, then they can give a little advice, but Mr. C. is the last to say anything of the faults of a child. I went before the Judge and there in the presence of that august body held up my hand and took the oath of administration but was not able to ascertain anything further as it regards the completion of business,

Last Thursday morn we were visited by the most severe earthquake that has been known for the last half century,[8] Those living

---

7. The insolvency of the great banking firm of Page, Bacon, and Co., in February, 1855, precipitated a drastic depression in San Francisco that affected the entire state. Many banking, express, and mercantile companies failed, the real estate market collapsed, and thousands of people were thrown out of work.

8. The earthquake occurred early in the morning of the 15th and lasted about ten seconds. It was felt even more severely at Oakland and extended as far south as Monterey. One account said the water rose in the Bay of San Francisco, maintained the higher level for five minutes, and then sank two feet below its ordinary state. Edward S. Holden, *Catalogue of Earthquakes on the Pacific Coast, 1769 to 1897* (Reprinted from the Smithsonian Miscellaneous collections No. 1087), p.46.

in high brick buildings fled to the streets and the plaza, but I was not at all frightened. Em was very anxious to get up, but I told her I should not, she thought she should take the next steamer home, but she seems more reconciled, I hear there are many going on that account, It seems to me in vain to shun the visitations of an overruling power; and I do not think we need look for another until another year. Many buildings were injured, mantel ornaments thrown down; those whose castors on their bedsteads played easily took a short ride across their room, much to their discomfort. The next day a deathlike stillness pervaded the city, never has there been such a suspension of business since the commencement of San Francisco.

Mrs Robinson does not enjoy the world as she would like, but looks forward to better days; she is obliged to practice the most rigid economy to live, but the Dr is full of hope that his claims will bring him a vast amount of gold whenever winter unbinds her chains in the mountains and gives them plenty of water, I think I told you of a little girl in the next house who strongly reminded me of Jennie, she is darker but her voice is the same. Her father and mother know nothing of bringing up a child and my heart aches for her that such a sweet face should not be made to show the cultivation of our better feelings. I feel that I should take her and make her a twin for Jennie if she had no other friend.

We have for the past week enjoyed the most beautiful weather; my muslins have been very acceptable; and the moon has been showing herself as she has not done for months before, All the city has been enjoying rides and walks. Mr Johnson took me out to the Ocean House. Had a large cream colored horse and a nice covered buggy; a very imposing team. Mr J. ordered dinner then we went on to the beach and rode about four miles along the shore where the waves rolled in from ten to twenty feet in height sometimes just reaching the horses feet, then they would seem we were floating, it would surround us in such a depth of water; a very singular sensation to not know which way you are going, then in a moment find yourself plodding on at the old pace. And every new form the waves chose to form themselves into, called a most ardent wish that you might enjoy, although you can see the ocean yet your view is limited to what it is here for hundred of miles one unbroken beach, in a calm quiet day such a heavy surf rolling it is truly sublime, A very sad accident occured the next day after we were there. A gentleman with two ladies, each a child, and servant, a span of horses a covered carriage were lost in the lake, which he undertook to cross, not knowing the way and seeing tracks he drove into the lake finding it getting too deep, in trying to retrace his steps all went down, down to unknown depths. The ladies babies, and horses were drowned, the man, and servant got on shore, but were unable to render any assistance as the carriage kept all beneath, a glove came to the surface torn and inside out, which told plainly of the anguish of a dying mother, but those cruel waters could not extinguish a mothers love for both were found with their babies clasped fast in their arms. They were Jews

And now for E[mily]. I have forborne saying anything of her, as it was her wish and it did seem hard that she could not be indulged in that, however injudicious she may have been, her situation was so trying one could but have sympathy for her, but I will give you an impartial account knowing you will keep it. We arrived at the dock and very soon her husbands brother came and said Sam would meet her at the Oriental Hotel, she told me it was because he did not like to have the meeting quite so public. Our clique had previously formed an engagement to all go to the International as it would be pleasant to be together, but E. wished me to go with her, so I made no objection but got into the carriage. On arriving at the Hotel I saw her pay her hack hire, then I felt all was not right. We went into the parlor no one came, such a feeling of loneliness crept over me, I thought I would not stay so I told E. she would be with Sam and I would go to the International which I did and found any number of friends. After dinner I asked a gentleman to walk down and see Emily with me. Found Sam sitting on the sofa, E. in the rocking chair, after an introduction I said Mr. B[arstow] you do not look happy, but he evaded an answer. I laughed and talked, then left wishing them joy. The next day I was in my agents office all the morning. When I came to the Hotel they told me Mr. Barstow refused to live with his wife. I went directly to see her, found her dressed in her best, looking as smiling as usual, as she said nothing of the affair I done the same and we walked out and told the friends it could not be, for she was as merry as ever. The next morning she sent for me to come and when I went into the room, she burst into tears and told me all and said the reason she did not do it before she was hoping he would relent. She told me he would be there in the evening and wished me to see him. I did so. The first word I said, was What is the trouble between you and Emily? He said: Mrs. Megquier, if you were a man I should tell you it was none of your business. I told him the relation I bore to her gave me the privilege of asking the question. Then he told me that Em. knew and he knew and that was sufficient. He then told me that he told her before he married that he did not love her when he saw her as he did when he was away, but as he promised he would fulfil but in every letter he had told her on no account to come to Cal unless she wished to be divorced. When he met her he sent his card to her room and she met him in the public parlor over a cold shake of the hand, not even the common kiss of friendships welcome greeted her and before an hour he told her they must be divorced. He told me he had not one spark of love for her and could not live with her but assigned no reason, was willing the world should think him the one to be blamed. He called on her because it was her request, but never for a moment relented. He sent a lawyer there before a week had passed to talk over the chances of getting a divorce. For desertion it would take two years, but they made adultery on his part the course and now she is free.

It is truly a strange freak. No one but expresses the deepest interest in her and I think she has received much more attention than she would under any other circumstances. I know of none who I think really love her but she receives much attention. Sam told her she had better go home and take George. She told him if she had wanted him she could have had before she came away. I thought that version of the story a little different from what I had heard at home. But I will say she has evinced some courage. She went alone into the court room to get copying and succeeded. They all take an interest in her some days she earns seven dollars but I think it wears upon her. Some mornings she really looks old but in the evening I think she is rather good looking. To prove the truth or falsity of what Charles said in his note I asked in an indifferent way, why she had never been a mother. She told me she miscarried once and for my part all proofs of the sex seem to be very prominent but often has the remark been made to me since I have been here it seemed so strange that Barstow could treat her in such a way unless there was something hidden. I have told you all I know but there is not a doubt but she knows what I do not, or she could not meet it as she does. And now I do not wish to add one wrong so you will keep this with you and Charles, for she has atoned for all injustice.

Now Charles I will tell you of a race I attended then I think you cannot accuse me of brevity. Last Tuesday I was down in town, when meeting Mr. J. he says The race comes off today, go in and take a lunch and we will go. We went and got a cup of tea, and toast, and took the cream with a fine buggy rode in to the ground but Mr. Johnson bet on the favorite horse so I would not come in but there was about four thousand at stake. One in the harness, the other under the saddle, Young America and Charley Speare. The first heat was 2.32, the next 2.22, the last they broke but decided in favor of the one in the harness, both paced. I enjoyed it there were two other ladies sat in the carriage with the back up where we could see the whole and to hear the "go it, Charley", "go it, America" was quite exciting but everything was as orderly as a meeting for fasting and prayer.

I am happy to have a line from you and it is in answer to your request that you get this long letter. I hope to see your handwriting often. Love to all but much to your little family. Tell Mary [Haskell] I will write her when I get one from her but I have so much that I cannot seem to get time only to answer. Kiss the little one and accept the best wishes of your Mother

SAN FRANCISCO, MARCH 4TH/56

Mr dear Angie
    Yours with baby in lap was received yesterday. I would like much to take Scottie while you were writing one letter, and now it seems

the time will be very short before I am with you. I have been turning my whole attention to thoughts of making a comfortable home here, but as it is impossible to have all here, I turn to make my arrangements to go home. The law says ten months, but I was before the Judge yesterday, he told me if t'was in his power he would make it less, I would like to be with you and the boys, but I dread the thought of returning. California life suits me, there is not a day I do not receive kind words and wishes of friends which are so very unlike what I will meet at home, excepting my children. Uncle Horace[9] was in last evening the same good looking man. I told him I hoped his negotiations would afford him money to go home when I did, he said No, he had not the least wish to ever visit New England again for there were none there that cared for him, had his mother lived, he would swim around Cape Horn to have seen her. A large tear rolled down his cheek without disturbing a muscle of his face. I blessed him for that. He gave me a genealogy he had picked up somewhere and wished me to send it to Aunt Angeline[10] to be inserted in the family bible but I have not time to write her therefore I send it to you to send her when an opportunity offers.

You write as though you felt some mortification attendant upon what has come upon us in the past few years. Now do not suffer it to give you a moments pain. We have a little circle of our own (and no one can intrude) with all the capabilities of being happy and so far am I from having any feeling about it I would not turn my hand over to have every thing blotted from the remembrance of the world, As for Emily I have told nothing that I would not tell the world. When she said hers was the hardest lost of any, I told her it was nothing to mine and all here knew how I was situated and do not for a moment blame and urge me to encourage you all to come where matters are looked upon in a different light from what they

---

9. Uncle Horace eventually returned to Norway and became a jeweler and watchmaker. He married Alice Denison (b. 1849) and had three children, born when he was in his forties. Lapham, *History of Norway*, p. 483. [1993]

10. Angeline Cole Sturtevant, a sister of Mary Jane's father, married to Noah Sturtevant and living in East Boston, Stackpole, *History of Winthrop*, p. 335. [1993]

are with you. I have many dear friends here and very much shall I regret leaving; if they are not sincere in what they say it makes one feel much happier to listen than to hear scandal dealt out to you from every quarter. Last Friday I spent the day at Mrs. Calkins. She took the trouble to provide my favorite dish, corned beef and cabbage. Mrs. Adams, Mrs. Davis were there. Mrs. D. has a beautiful boy but he has some organic affection which is liable to take him off at any time tears coursed down her cheeks when she nursed him to think she must part with him their little girl is a perfect beauty. They told me the Shaw girls were all going into the western country. Edith I see very often, she makes an excellent housewife and has acquired a station which many with more talent and money might seek for in vain. Mr. Johnson of whom you have heard me speak, is a worthy friend of mine, he has built a new house for his brother and boards with them. He takes a great interest in you and says he shall give you a call when he goes home, he thinks you are a much better woman than your Mother, but says he will go to the end of the world to please me, we are all invited to make him a call Friday night. How I would like to have you and Charles there. I saw Mr. Snell yesterday. He inquired for you all. Says tell Charles nothing would afford him more pleasure than a ride after that fast nag. I am still at Mrs. Robinsons who speaks of you as one of her dearest friends. She talks of those days in Maine as among her happiest. I think she enjoys our society for it brings her many calls and I have the vanity to think the gentlemen of our acquaintance are quite as interesting as any in the city.

Last night we had a fine time, we played euchre until half past ten then we went to Winns. I took waffles and coffee the rest omelettes, and dry toast. It is quite as far from us as from your house to Browns garden on Bramhalls Hill and where they are grading it is worse traveling than on those loose stones which we travelled over in going to Mount Washington but you know that I can laugh it all off and make them think it first rate. Mr. Dorman the brother is here who you saw at Monmouth, he says it is strange you cannot send a little love to him. I told him I would mention it to you but he will probably be in the states before I get an answer to this. I shall send you a picture, if I have any money when he goes. It will be for Jennie, but I suppose she will hand it to her friends. It is strange Bettie does not write either of us I expected a long letter from her but not one word from Winthrop, it is strange when not a mail goes without taking two or three from me. But I can live without them as yet. Now love to all and tell Charles I prize his letters highly. Much love to you and the babies.

Mother

SAN FRANCISCO MAR 19TH

My dear Angie,

I received only one letter last mail, that from Mr. Gilson, from New York, and two from Winthrop which ought to have been here the mail previous. I assure you I retrace my steps with a heavy heart when I get no word from you, or the boys, but I think it must be some detention of the mail as Emily received none. I am still waiting like Macawber. I sometime think I will sell, for just what I can get and go home, but I should be miserable indeed, without money but I have not much to do, and were it not that we had many calls I should be most homesick, but, there is ever something to kill time, I have been to a party at Mr Johnsons since I wrote you; given in that new house he has been building. It is furnished in fine style and the refreshments were of the most delicious kind. We had strawberries put up in France, champagne in abundance, one little unique bottle stood in the centre of the table neatly encased in straw, with a little glass which would take a table spoonful to fill, which I found was for me, it was a kind of cordial as smooth as oil, with no intoxicating quality. I felt I was kindly cared for, as it no doubt took a good smart five to buy it, if not ten. We had bon bons in abundance which in pulling apart sudenly explode like torpedoes, no doubt arises from the vast amount of sentiment they contain. We had two fiddlers which made the time pass merrily indeed. Night before last we went to a little quadrille party at Mrs Martins, Yesterday I spent the day with Mrs Davis She has two beautiful babies she says I shall have a picture of little Annie to take home. We had two tables of euchre, between eleven and twelve we had tea made from the flower of tea, which I assure you was fit for the Gods; served in little cups the size of an hens egg, fancy cakes, nuts and raisans, she wished to be remembered to you. We were at Mrs. Adams to lunch last week. Had beef steak, corned beef, boiled eggs, blanche mange, pies. Mrs. Adams told me if I would spend the evening, I should have a dance, but the Captain of the Steamship Cortez called with a gentleman who I knew was there and wished me to go home, that he could see Emily, so I gave up the dance but I was astonished to hear that from Mrs. Adams.

We are having delightful weather now but they fear a great amount of suffering if there is no more rain, the miners can get no water to wash their gold. The Dr. [Robinson] writes very flattering, if he can only get water she is looking forward to the indulgence of a moire antique to promenade Montgomery Street I really wish she could get it, for she is really deserving and you have a firm friend in her.

Emily is writing with me. It does not seem possible that she will do me any injustice for she never says ill of any one. I think she is easily influenced and very proud, but she does wish to support herself she has very many friends.

Give love to Hattie and tell her I see some of the Webbs every day Dr. Gibbons is very homesick but the others are well and comparatively happy. I had a line from Lizzie Sears.[11] She tells me John is steady and home nearly every evening. I hope Charles will advise about the farm for I cannot know what is best. Mr. Snell says there is not a man in Maine he would be more happy to see. I do want to be with you but I dread sitting myself down in Winthrop. Remember me to Charles H[askell] and Mary, your Charles and the dear little ones and know you are ever in my thoughts. With all a Mother's love

Jen

---

11. Elizabeth Sears lived next door in Winthrop. The Megquiers bought some land and water rights from the Sears family. [1993]

My dear Angie

No doubt I told you in my last how much I was disappointed in not hearing from you but this mail made amends by bringing two, giving a very good account of your winters entertainment. I suppose if I should be so happy as to be with you another winter, there shall be nothing of the kind. It seems to me I shall have a dull time indeed, only when you can be with me. Milton no doubt will entertain me Sunday evenings. We have a visitor here a friend of Mr Robinsons who discourses Byron splendidly, it is truly an intellectual treat, and he is full of jokes, so that our Sabbath evenings are spent as they should be, pleasantly.

I have been to hear the minstrels since I wrote you last, they sing some beautiful ballads which takes me directly to you, nothing can do it so effectually as music. I went with Mr Johnson Mrs Robinson with a Mr Bostwick a friend of mine Em. was engaged and did not go. We went to Mr Johnsons had a mince pie a glass of champagne and a nice dance after the performance was over, which brought it into the small hours before we retired which does not affect the subscriber at all, but Mrs R. cannot endure dissapation. Last night we went to hear the Gougenhimes.[12] The manager of the Union theatre lives next door to us and gave us the use of a private box. Mrs R's brother was all the gentlemen we had, who by the way is the greatest tease in the world and we had more fun among ourselves than on the stage, it rained in torrents when we came home and Orin joked Mrs Robinson so hard she has not been herself to day, she is certainly the most delicate woman and she ought to have a husband that would shield her from the slightest touch of this cold and heartless world but it is not so, and I can think of nothing but a water lily crushed by some rude hand, she is not as pretty as when you saw her yet she has a beautiful skin and curls her hair in front

---

12. The Gougenheim sisters, Adelaide and Josy, came to San Francisco direct from Paris late in 1855 and opened a highly successful engagement of sixteen nights at the Metropolitan under the management of Joseph French. Phillips, *Portsmouth Square*, p. 352.

and fastens it with that same gold arrow as in olden time. One week her husband will write her that his prospects are such as promise him gold to make them above the petty annoyance that have troubled them; the next says the D[evil] is in it and she is clouds, and sunshine just as his letters dictate. Emily is writing as usual and thus far we are as happy a family as can be found, only that I feel I ought to be looking after those boys, but Arthur and Bettie both say John is steady. I do think Miller will some day be repaid for his unkind insinuations but just give me an independence with my children and I care not for any, I know I can be as happy as the majority.

It has been very hard times here and many predicted famine, but for the last few days it has been raining and if it gives water to the miners it will be better times, and I shall sell the first offer and make the best of my way home, yet I sincerely regret leaving this country, it is the place to enjoy life. Poor Bettie, there seems to be none to bear with her but me and for her Mother's sake, I shall do all in my power to make her comfortable, and if Milton will read to me and keep me informed on political subjects, he shall have a piece of pie when there is any. She write me the same as ever, but does not mention you, she feels there is something wrong, no doubt, somewhere; but I think she will do all to make you happy in Winthrop, if not she will receive a censure from me for I love to think of you there enjoying yourselves, and how much would I like to step in and look upon you there, John and Arthur playing their pranks and you laughing at them, but I cannot dwell upon it for it makes me unhappy. I thought of them often yesterday [April 1st], in their efforts to fool each other. And now I would bring you here to this same window that I have before told you of, there are a dozen big clippers unlading their freight of boxes, and barrels, pails, and wash tubs, I see now a pile of pails as big as this house and who knows but they come from Turner. The Sacramento boats are just going out three of them and I can hear every revolution of the wheel as they pass the window, When the last steamer went to the states the Captain and Engineer stood on the wheel house and waived their handkerchiefs to us, we were ironing so we took a sheet and returned the salute. I know not what more to write, therefore I will leave until the fourth.

APRIL 4TH.

Yesterday Mrs Robinson, Emily and myself started for a walk out of town, took a lunch at a fried of Ems from New York with the addition of two ladies from there and two gents, we walked to the mission, visiting a number of private gardens which are perfectly splendid now: roses, verbenas fucias and gillyflowers seem to predominate but the verbenas surpass any thing I ever saw, clusters as large as a teacup, of every shade covering quite an extent of ground, you could but be happy while gazing upon them. In looking upon the roses I saw a most beautiful bud one side the deepest red, the other a blush but I thought it would be selfish to ask for it, so I left with it only impressed upon my memory, but before I left the garden a gentleman brought it to me. I thought it quite singular, it is now in a glass on the table. I wish it could go to you with all its freshness, We went and took an ice cream came home well satisfied with the days adventure. I will now leave enjoying the thought there is one less to write before I see you. I hope to see Charles friendly handwriting before long. With much love to all. Remember me to Mother. I dreamed of her last night. Be of good cheer, I shall be with you soon.

Your Mother J.M.

I have written Dr. Perkins this mail.

SAN FRANCISCO MAY 4TH

My dear Angie
Never since I have left you have I felt I had so little to write about as now. After Dr Robinson come from the mines I felt that Mrs R, could do without us; I accepted the invitation of Mrs Calkins to come and stay with her awhile as Mrs Davis had gone to housekeep-

Surrender of James P. Casey and Charles Cora, May 18, 1856.

ing, she wanted my company, And now we have a nice sitting room,
and bed room, which makes it very pleasant. I assist Mrs C. in
sewing to pay my way for awhile, but I do hope the day is not far
distant when I can dispose of what little interest there is here and
go home, for I do want to be with you although I do like the society
far better here than home, and shall have many lonely hours when

I return, Bettie tells me she cannot stay with the boys much longer and I really think she is to be married for John says Milton is there three times a week and stays all night. Milton wrote me he thought he[13] should be able to introduce me to Mrs. Benjamin when I return. Bettie complains of being lonely but how much more real will be her loneliness when she is bound to a man for whom she has not sympathies, she thinks she loves him, but she will find that she cannot appreciate what there is lovable in him, he will take to his business, and reading, she to her calls and what little gossip there is going. I really pity her for she knows not what she is taking upon herself.

Dr Robinson is remodelling his play of the past, present, and future, and Mrs R. is again picturing to herself genteel hats, charmant satins, mantel of the same, lined with white silk, it seems to me, her face is lighted up as readily as little Jens when you tell her some little story, never was there a match where there were two greater extremes than in theirs, He cannot make an assertion without confirming it with an oath, which grates so harshly upon her ear that she begs of him to desist, when he will make some witty remark which drives every pain from her breast, and she feels proud to look upon him and call him hers,

Mr Dorman wishes to be remembered to you, he can call many things to mind which he thinks you inherit from your Mother. He is a fine young man but his associations with Dr Robinson is enough to contaminate any one that is intimately connected with him, but Dorman is a noble hearted man has no bad habits; but cannot feel any interest in any business matters, but what appertains in some way to theatricals, a business which I detest unless I could be a star of first magnitude, The church bells are ringing, it sounds very pleasant to me, we were so far from them at Mrs Robinsons that they often rang unnoticed by me, Tell Jen I see a little girl her style,

---

13. Bettie L. Benjamin married John Milton Benjamin on July 2, 1856. The Chinese sewing box given to Bettie by the Megquiers was passed down to their daughter, Fannie Benjamin Herrick, who passed it down to her daughter, Marjory Herrick, who gave it to Gilson descendants. Stackpole, *History of Winthrop*, pp. 279–80. See page 164. [1993]

going past with a little pink silk hat, set jauntily on the top of her head, a dark blue thibet coat, with two bright plaid stripes of some material around the skirt, and she looks into her papas face and says some happy thing, I wish I could have her here for a few days, we would be as happy as they, There is nothing in this country I wish more for you to see than the flowers, they partake of the spirit of the inhabitants for being fast, very fast, yesterday I saw a rose that would fill a large sized pint bowl, it was sitting outside a store. I stopped to examine thinking there might be two, you may be assured I thought of you, I thank you kindly for such a nice long letter and should give you eight pages in return, but having so many to answer I will divide between you and Mary, knowing you will share together. I received two from Portland, and six from W[inthrop] all of which I shall answer and nothing in the world to say.

The last steamer came in about four in the afternoon, knowing the mail would open about ten in the evening, I made the remark I should go down, nothing more was said at the time, Two gentlemen came in the evening we talked over the news from the states, then commenced my favorite game of euchre, when ten oclock came, I threw down my cards, and rushed up stairs for my hat, and shawl, went into the room, and asked if any of the gentlemen were going down in town, they looked at each other, and I just turned on my heel and was off, it was not that they did not wish to go, but they did not wish to interfere and I had a nice time travelling such an outlandish street that is not lighted for three quarters of a mile alone, in such a place as this, but I rushed through a crowd of hundreds, a privilege a lady has, got my letters and got home in twenty-five minutes, but I felt cross as a bear but said not a word. They told me I was too hasty I told them that was my business, just like me you will say. You ask when Mr. Johnson is going home, sometime this fall, but I hope to be there before him, if not, he will come and see you, he is a perfect gentleman. Emily had an invite to go to the islands which she thinks she shall accept the next trip. I shall miss her much. Love to all especially your own household, the dear little ones I do wish much to see. I hope you will have a long and happy visit to Winthrop. With the love of an absent Mother

Jennie

[M AY 1 8 5 6][14]

My dear Jennie,

I send you a picture as it is within one block of your grandmother it may please you The carriage is the one the prisoner was taken in. Tell Scottie all about it, and instill into his little mind it is best to be good and not tease his sister.

Your Grandmother Jennie

SAN FRANCISCO JUNE 19TH,

My dear Angie

Yours of the 20th of May is at hand, and as ever gives me pleasure to read. We were in a great muss when last I wrote, but now we are nicely esconsed in one of the finest houses in S.F. Emily and myself have a fine room in the third story overlooking the city. We have a neat bed in one corner with a white Marsailles quilt, and a mosquito net, very well arranged which makes it look very cosy, We have a dressing table, with two large pitchers, two mugs for teeth, two boxes of tooth paste, and two looking glasses one high, and one low, brushes, and combs, in the drawer, Then we have a

---

14. This note was written on the inside sheet of the pictorial notepaper reproduced on p. 160. Here and in the following letter Mrs. Megquier refers to the Vigilance Committee of 1856 and the threatened "war" between the Vigilantes or Citizens and the regularly constituted officials, supported by the so-called "Law and Order" men. The Committee, usually referred to as the Second Vigilance committee, was organized immediately following the shooting of James King of William, editor of the San Francisco *Bulletin*. On May 18 a body of 3,000 armed men, representing the Committee, took Charles Cora and James P. Casey, King's assailant, from the San Francisco jail and brought them before the Committee's tribunal for trial. The men were condemned and executed the day of King's funeral.

CHINESE SEWING BOX, GIFT FROM THE MEGQUIERS TO BETTIE AND
MILTON BENJAMIN, 1850S [1993].

nice black walnut wardrobe, a mahogany round table with a lamp,
books, and flowers for ornament, then a little table for euchre, a
lounge, chairs make up the furniture, Never in my life did I live as
free as now, I have a fine circle of friends, sew for Mrs Calkins to
pay my board, I rent the building for a trifle enough to find me in
what I must have, but amidst all I know how much the boys need
my care, and I am going to sell in a few weeks but if it does not
bring enough to pay the debts and take me home, I shall have to
bid it in, and still wait for better times.[15]

No doubt you will feel very anxious about me, when you read of
the state of things existing here. We look upon tomorrow as big
with the fate of this unfortunate city. I cannot be frightened but

15. In the end, the lawyer who settled Richmond's estate gave Mary Jane Megquier only
enough money for her passage home and to pay board. "Citation to Mary J. Megquier, Adm.,
March 1860." Thomas L. Megquier estate, Registry of Probate, Kennebec County. [1993]

many can neither eat, nor sleep, they say the law and order people will plunder and burn the city, and there is no knowing what will become of the women, and children, I assure you it looks very like war, to go through our streets in the evening and see thousand [of] bayonets glimmering in the moonlight going through their different evolutions, every one showing a determination to carry their point, Never was such a state of things known to exist in any country, when a body of men met together and took the law in their own hands, and sit night and day looking into the frauds that have been practiced here, and the first thing some one has orders to leave. Some say they will do so others throw themselves under the protection of the former rulers and say they will try titles, As the steamer goes tomorrow it will decide who rules, The vigilance have cannon faced in every direction and bags of sand piled around to defend those that fire the cannon,[16] it is said they have five thousand; while the other party have not more than one, I shall be glad when it is decided for such a state of things suspends all business and makes it decidedly bad for me, but you will find a better account in the papers than I can give.

Dr. Robinson is going home this mail he had a benefit at the Union theatre which gave him a pretty sum, he says he shall go to see you. I had my face put into a case which I send by him, for Jennie, every one says it is perfect. I want you to send it to Winthrop on a short visit as I fondly hope there are a few who would like to look at it. I told him if he was detained in New York to send it on by express. I had a letter from Mary Annah inviting me to Sacramento she says Augusta is married.[17] I think she must like the country better than when she first came. We are to have an opening party next week if we do not all get killed. I have got me a white muslin and Emily wears her lemon silk, You may think I speak rather slightly but you can get familiar

---

16. The Committee had 9,000 members, a fortified headquarters known as Fort Gunnybags, and a well-equipped arsenal.

17. Mary Annah and Augusta were John Quincy Cole's sisters. Stackpole, *History of Winthrop*, p. 334. [1993]

with any thing. The states quartermaster says he has marked me and is going to pop at me the first one. I tell him to fire away, he cannot get ammunition enough to reach the third story. All my friends are of the vigilance committee but him, he is one of 42, and has been in the service of the state but I think he is sick of his bargain.

I do hope you and Mary [Haskell] will go to Winthrop[18] and stay two months. I think you might enjoy it you could manage to suit yourselves, take the house in your own hands and have a good time, it would give the boys so much pleasure. Lizzie [Sears] says she fears you did not enjoy yourself when last there. I should hope you would not allow Bettie to mar your happiness, for I am sure she could not mine on my own premises. I wish when you write to East Boston you would say to the Doct. I have written him three times, and only received one short note from him. Give love to Mary. Tell her I see Mrs. Hubbard often, she enjoys life finely, she goes to dinners twice a week, has often invited me and if nothing prevents think I shall go next Saturday eve.

Had a line from Mr. Gibson he speaks well of you but you said nothing of him. The lunch bell is ringing. I wish you could be here for it is free and easy, all the other meals we are obliged to be dressed in better shape. We dine at seven in the evening and then comes the frolic and dancing. Shant I miss them at home. I shall have the blues but I shall not repine if the boys[19] are only

---

18. The mortgage on the house was cleared soon after Mary Jane Megquier returned to Winthrop in 1856. Mary Jane was given a "life interest" in one-third of the property and the three children divided the remaining two-thirds among them. In 1861, John and Arthur each sold their portions to Mary Jane, leaving Mary Jane and Angie the joint owners of the property. Russell B. Norton to Mary J. Megquier et al., 16 October 1856, Book 208, p. 172; John O. Megquier to Mary Jane Megquier and Arthur S. Megquier to Mary Jane Megquier, 5 November 1861, Book 228, pp. 513–14, Kennebec County Registry of Deeds. [1993]
19. John Otis Megquier was a machinist and iron worker and died in 1907. His wife, Mattie, died in 1877. Arthur Selwyn Megquier served in the Civil War and, after working in New York City, established the firm of Megquier & Jones, dealers in brass castings and structural iron work, in Portland. He married Adelaide Hall of Brooklyn, NY, in 1868 and they had two daughters. He died in 1891. Maine Vital Records; Little, *Genealogical and Family History of the State of Maine*, p. 625. Thanks to Patti Lincoln for her search of the Maine Vital Records. [1993]

steady. Give love to all. Tell Jennie I send her the picture that she may not forget me. Tell Mother of my good health whenever you have a chance and hope I may have some thing more pleasant to write next time. My thanks for Charles letter

    With much love to yourself

Mother

INDEX

April Fools' Day, 158

Barrett, Sam, 83, 94, 95, 100, 135
Barstow, Emily, xix
  finds work, 151–52
  tries to reunite with husband, 141,
    150–52
Batchelder, Andrew, 44
Batchelder, Henry, 89, 92
Beechcroft (Megquier house in
  Winthrop, ME), xxi, 144, 166
Beede and Bodge stage line, 87, 89, 101,
  106–7
Benjamin, Bettie L., 3, 6, 40, 77, 166
  marriage, 3n, 121
Benjamin, J. Milton, 1n, 102, 147, 157
  marriage, 3n, 121
Benson, Julia, 66
Benson, Sewall, 117
Biscaccianti, Elise, 107
  boarding houses, xivn, xvii–xviii,
    xxix, 68–69, 72, 97–99, 122
Bowdoin College, xiv
Boynton, Dr. J.F., 59
Bradford Academy, 66
Brinsmade, P.A., 6, 16
Budd, Capt. Thomas S., 10, 17, 20

California
  crops in, 109
  interest rates in, 49n
  politics, 43, 51, 98

California (ship), 34n
Calkin, Mr. (agent), 9, 14, 16, 26, 29,
  41, 45–46, 63, 83, 85, 105
Calkin, Mrs., 116, 121, 135, 142, 154,
  160
Casey, James P., 160, 163n
Castillo rapids, 80, 140
Chagres, 12–14, 28
Chapman, Caroline, 130–31
Chinese community, 86
Clay, Henry
  death of, 97
Cole, Hiram (uncle of MJM), 58
Cole, Horace (brother of MJM), 21
Cole, Horatio (uncle of MJM), 27n,
  36
Cole, John and Sarah (uncle and aunt of
  MJM), 87
Cole, John Quincy (cousin of MJM),
  36, 73, 83, 114, 165n
Cole, Mary Annah (cousin of MJM),
  114, 165
Cole, Nathan (father of MJM), 1n,
  108
Cole, Rebecca Pollard (mother of
  MJM), xiii–xiv, 10
  letter by, 83–84
  religion of, xiv, 126
Cole, "Uncle" Horace (cousin of MJM),
  27n, 36, 48, 57, 83, 96, 97, 99,
  114, 120, 143
  returns to Maine, 153n

schemes for making fortune, 125
in shipwreck, 118
Cora, Charles, 160, 163n

Davis, Mrs. R.D.W., 87, 115, 121, 123
142, 155–156
Davis, R.D.W., 10, 39, 83

earthquake, 148

Farmington, ME, 53
fires, 54, 63–66, 110
floods, 50, 110
Forni, José, 106n, 111
Fremont, Jessie Benton, xxivn, 32n

Gardiner, Capt., 26
Gilson, Angeline L. (daughter of MJM
and TLM), xxi, 2n, 166n
marriage, xv, 75
Gilson, Anne (daughter of ALG and
CAG), xxi, 147n
Gilson, Arthur Scott (son of ALG and
CAG)
birth, 147n
Gilson, Charles A. (husband of ALG),
75n, 77, 156
marriage, xv, 75n
Gilson, Charles (son of ALG and CAG),
147n
Gilson, Henry Clinton (son of ALG and
CAG), 147n
Gilson, Jennie. See Wilder, Jennie
Gilson
Gilson, Marjary. See Lund, Marjary
Gilson
gold mining machines, 7n
Gold Rush, 21, 24, 31–32, 35, 37–38,
41–42
Gorgona, 15–19, 30
Gorham Academy, xiv
Gougenheim, Adelaide and Josy, 157

Greytown, 80
Grimes, H., 59

Haines, Joseph A., 47
Hartwell, John, 44n
Haskell, Charles H., 3, 4, 21, 59, 69
Haskell, Mary, 4
Hawes, Howard, 72n
Hayes, Kate, 105, 113, 126
Herz, Henri, 55
horse races, 152

ice cream parlor, 121, 159
Ilsley, Capt. Frederick, 27n, 62
Ilsley, Mrs. Frederick, 27, 60, 65, 71,
93, 96
Independence
lost in 1852, 119

Lake Nicaragua, 80, 140
Lee, Capt., 79–80
Lund, Marjary Gilson (daughter of
ALG and CAG), xxi, 147n

Maine natives in California, xvii, 30, 48, 60,
65, 83, 87, 89, 92–93, 96, 117, 133
Mann, Capt., 63, 67, 88, 96, 104, 115,
135
loses ship, 118
Mazuka rapids, 80, 140
Megquier, Angeline L. See Gilson,
Angeline L.
Megquier, Arthur Selwyn (son of MJM
and TLM), xv, 2n, 166n
Megquier, James, 60
Megquier, John (of Poland, ME), xxiiin
Megquier, John Otis (son of MJM and
TLM), 5, 44, 52–53, 120, 156, 166n
Megquier, Mary Jane
anxiety about children, xvii, 37
arrives in San Francisco, 35–36, 82,
139

at Chagres, 10–13
at Panama, 16–32
birth and childhood, xiii–xiv
builds house in Winthrop, ME, xix,
136
crosses Isthmus of Panama, xvi–xvii,
14–17, 28–30
crosses Nicaragua, 79–81, 139–41
death of, xxi
decides to go to California, xvi, 3, 6
describes lodgings, 112–13
feelings about returning to Maine,
141, 160, 166
finds freer life in San Francisco, 56,
120, 148, 153, 157, 160, 164, 166
makes clothes, xvi, 9, 64
makes profit in pickles, 43
marriage, xiv
misses family, xviii–xix, 64, 104, 107,
116, 120, 124–25, 127, 131, 141,
153, 162
needlework by, xi
problems with husband, xix, 143–44
religion of, xiv, 1, 56, 68
returns home from first journey, 75
returns home from second journey,
133n
returns to Maine for good, xv, xx,
166–67
runs boarding house, xvii–xviii, 53,
68–69, 72, 97–99, 122
sails on *Northern Light,* 75
sails on *Oregon,* 34–35
sews for living, 160
social life in San Francisco, xvii, 54,
57, 60, 64–65, 70–71, 73, 133,
154–55, 166
Megquier, Thomas L.
advises daughter about health, 136
alone in San Francisco, 135–37
ancestry of, xxiiin, xxviii
builds house in San Francisco, 124, 132

builds house in Winthrop, ME, xvii,
75n
death of, xix–xx, 144n
education of, xiv
and farm in Maine, 102–3, 116
practices medicine in Panama, 25, 31
practices medicine in San Francisco,
xviii, 43, 96
problems with partner and partner's
estate, 84–85, 88, 91, 108–9
reasons for going to California, 8
sends gold or money home, 58, 69–
70, 100
sickness of, 58, 63, 97, 115, 139n, 144
Merrill family, xxiiin
mines, 27, 42, 156
Montez, Lola, xxx, 128–29
Morrill, John, 100, 102–16

Nicaragua route, xxix, 79–81, 139–141
North America
lost in 1852, 76
Northerner, 10
Northern Light, 75

Ocean House, 141, 149
Odd Fellows, xvi, 4
Oregon, 34

Pacific, 82
Panama, 16–32, 30–31
Panama route, xxviii, 10–32, 12n
Plume, Atty., 91, 124, 164n

Reynolds, Mary T., 2, 4, 21, 61, 88
Reynolds, Oliver, 4, 57, 59, 66, 71, 87
Richmond, Cyrus C., 16, 38, 48, 83–85
death of, 88
estate settled, 164
partner to Thomas L. Megquier, 3n
Richmond, Mrs. Cyrus C., 3n, 83–84,
103, 105

Robinson, Dr. D.G., xxx, 59, 62, 65, 115, 121–22, 147
  at the mines, 142, 147, 149, 159
  benefit for, 130–31, 165
  boards with Megquiers, 83, 86
  new play, 161
  opens theater, 70
  sells patent medicine, 92

Sacramento
  fires, 110
  floods, 50
San Francisco
  in 1849, 39, 42
  churches, 56, 135–36
  depression in, 148n
  earthquake, 148–49
  fires, 54, 63, 65–66
  politics, 51–52, 60, 72, 96–98
  prices in, 35, 39, 42, 50, 109
  printers in, 55n
  public execution in, 106
  social life, 54, 65, 70, 73, 155
Sears, Elizabeth, 156
Sears, Susan, 101
Sears, Thomas, 103
Severance, Luther, 48
shipwrecks, 45, 76, 118, 119

Sinclair, Catherine, xxx, 126
Sturtevant, Angeline Cole, 153n

Taboga, island of, 22–23
Tewksbury, Jacob, 46, 93, 96
theaters, 50, 157
Turner, ME, 1, 117, 119
  first Baptist church in, 1n

Vanderbilt
  oversells voyages, 76–78
Vigilance Committees, 51, 106, 163, 165
Virgin Bay, 80, 140

Walker, William, 140n
Wiggin, Capt., 72
Wilder, Jennie Gilson (daughter of ALG and CAG), xxii
  birth, xviii, 104n
Winthrop, ME, xiv, xv, xix, 134–35, 144, 166
women
  and importance of familial ties, xii, xv, xxi
  and role in family decisions, xvi
  work of valued, xvii, 3, 146
women singers and actresses, xxx, 105, 107, 113, 126, 128–29, 130–31, 157